Trapped in America

BY JERRY LOW

Published by EDK Books and
Distributed by EDK Distribution, LLC
edkbooksanddistribution.com
edkbooksanddistribution@gmail.com | (206) 227-8179

Trapped in America
Copyright © 2022 by Jerry Low

All rights reserved. No part of this book may be reproduced, stored in, or introduced into a retrieval system, or transmitted in any form, or by any means (electronic, mechanical, photocopying, recording, or otherwise) without the prior written permission of the publisher, except in the case of brief quotations in articles or critical reviews.

Unless otherwise indicated, quotes from Scripture are from the New King James Version (NKJV)

ISBN: 978-1-956065-10-7

Library of Congress Control Number: 2022910852

Cover photograph: Genna Sidler
Cover design-book layout: Julie K. Lee @ Lee Creative
Editor: Barbara Kindness

Printed in the United States of America

10 9 8 7 6 5 4 3 2 1

Dedication

To Zuzanna and our three children
– Asa, Gordon, and Joy –
Treasures beyond Measure

Acknowledgments

My sincere gratitude to three special families
– the Wilks, Griffings, and Millers –
whose friendship, support, and endless devotion to
our missionary life made this a journey ever-uplifting,
ever-brimming with God's love.

CONTENTS

INTRODUCTION xiii

PART ONE: Lost – And Found
Chapter One 3
Chapter Two 7
Chapter Three 11
Chapter Four 15
Chapter Five 23
Chapter Six 27
Chapter Seven 33
Chapter Eight 41

PART TWO: New Mission, New Life
Chapter Nine 45

PART THREE: Life in Yugoslavia
Chapter Ten 65
Chapter Eleven 75

PART FOUR: Trapped in America
Chapter Twelve 83
Chapter Thirteen 93
Chapter Fourteen 113

PART FIVE: Back to a Dream

Chapter Fifteen 121
Chapter Sixteen 137
Chapter Seventeen 149

PART SIX: Sabbatical

Chapter Eighteen 181

PART SEVEN: New Year, New Decade

Chapter Nineteen 191

PART EIGHT: Trapped in America – Again

Chapter Twenty 199

ENDORSEMENTS

Jerry Low lived his life captivated by two things—prayer and the love of missions. A man of humble beginnings and early rebellion against God and authorities, Jerry changed. He made an absolute about face. Jesus turned his life around by the power of His cross, death, and resurrection. This is precisely why Jerry became a man of prayer and a lover of the nations.

We had the privilege of being sent out from Shady Grove Church in the early 1980s with a couple of short-term trips to Eastern Europe. Jerry was on those teams. This was in the early 1980s before the Iron Curtain fell. It was in this adventure and upon the fertile soil of Soviet peoples that we really got to know the heart of Jerry for God and for the Gospel. On one of those trips he met his wife-to-be, Zuzanna. Little did we know how those early outreach endeavors would greatly impact Jerry's life, the calling of our church in missions, and eventually other nations.

As we traveled from church to church, we encountered hungry people, longing to know more—to receive solid Bible training. When it was Jerry's turn to speak, the audience perked up and leaned forward, straining to digest every word. He had a story to tell of how Jesus saved and delivered him from drugs and a hard life enslaved to the rigors of sin. Jerry told that story over and over throughout his life, in other nations, and to many people.

There was a real move of God in the 1980s and '90s in the small, out-of-the-way church in Grand Prairie, Texas—Shady Grove. Sunday after Sunday, the glory of God poured down as the congregation worshipped. The manifest presence of God was tangible, like lightning flashing through the people who lifted their faces to see the image of God each week in that glorious place. It was there that Jerry and Zuzanna Low were prepared to be released, eventually, back to Eastern Europe. They spent two decades-plus under the leadership and discipleship of Pastor Olen Griffing and, at the time, missions pastor Monty Smith. And the more we all worshipped together, the more leadership released dozens into the mission field. The closer we came to know and understand the heart of God, the more we loved the lost. The world was wide open and many were coming and going. A vast number of seeds were sown in those days, and people willingly gave from their pockets and from their hearts. People packed their bags and wanted to participate in making disciples throughout the world.

Jerry and Zuzanna Low had a key part in this. It was there they raised their three children, and it was there that something wonderful was deposited for the thrusting out of their calling to the Balkans. At times, this training seemed to pass slowly. Jerry and Zuzanna became eager to be sent out permanently as missionaries. But they were patient to stay the course until God's time was right. It was their persistent and disciplined prayer life that sustained them until that day. Only Heaven will tell of the seeds that have been sown. Heaven will reveal the answers to prayers on bended knees. The weeping over the rich and ripe harvest that happened in their hearts will be shown in fruit on that day.

It has been a privilege to know them and walk with them throughout life. It has not been a surprise to see them blossom and begin to bear fruit in Eastern Europe where their lives together began. It has been awesome to see them come full circle. And it has been an honor to cheer them forward as champions in God's kingdom.

We highly recommend this book. *Trapped in America* is a portrait of a man whose life was healed under the powerful hand of God's redemption through Jesus. It is the legacy of a man that understood the heart of God because he prayed. It is a story of a man that developed a passion for the Gospel to be spread around the world, pure and simple. You will be impacted by his story and compelled to see what he saw as he traveled and told his story over and over.

Oswald Chambers said, "Prayer does not equip us for greater works, prayer is the greater work." Jerry Low understood this and not only understood it—but did it! It drove him to spend his life in the harvest field of world missions.

His message is compelling and challenging, "Pray and Go." And that is what he did. Most of all, Jesus can be seen in his choices. We are very grateful for his life and for the lives of this devoted family.

— **Dr. Wayne and Bonnie Wilks,**
Pastor Wayne Wilks is an executive pastor over Jewish ministry at Gateway Church, and Bonnie is the author of the book *Sabbath: a Gift of Time*

Who is Jerry Low for us? He is a man who, by his example, encouraged a deeper relationship with the Lord, who could at times put us to shame with his devotion to the vision of expanding the Kingdom of God in the Balkans. We learned from him the value of remaining in the hidden and the value of background work, prayer and immersion in God's presence. We are honored to have had the opportunity to know Jerry and share many precious times of prayer with him!

— **Bartol and Biljana Pešorda,**
Founders of Dom molitve – Slavonski Brod in Croatia

I would like to sing you some stories.

Would you listen for a while?

I can't really promise you they will all make you smile.

Only how you listen. Are you listening at all?

It's all in if you want to learn or do you know it all?

• • • • •

Every life's a story. Every life is a song.

Some will live in Glory, and some never will belong.

Everyone could write a book that others could learn from.

So, I want you please to listen to the stories in my life's song.

• • • • •

I would like to sing you some stories; maybe you could sing for me.

Maybe we will communicate and more of love we'll see.

Let's try to be honest and not play the usual games.

Let's learn from those before, from their laughter and their pain.

© Karen Lafferty

INTRODUCTION

I actually love America, and as you read this book you will understand the title. I am glad to be an American and I am especially blessed to have been born in Texas. On my mother's side of the family, I am a fifth or sixth generation Texan (according to how you count the length of a generation). My father's side of the family came to Texas in the late 1800s. I can truthfully say I am a Texas American.

Let me apologize, I am not a wordsmith. This book is not colored with eloquent writings to stimulate the senses, rather I have written as I talk. I do feel you will enjoy the many adventures I have had the privilege to walk through.

Back to the title and the main reasons for writing the book. The title springs from a passion God gave me in 1975. That passion has driven my life for all these years—giving me a purpose to live for, hope to dream of, and it has taken me into the most interesting situations and places. In my early Christian life God gave me a verse that I have felt and seen over and over:

Matt. 6:33 But seek ye first the kingdom of God, and His righteousness; and all these things shall be added unto you." (KJV)

This verse is from Jesus' discourse on the mountainside to his disciples. Jesus was speaking about the needs of this life saying;

Matt. 6:25 "Therefore I say to you, do not worry about your life, what you will eat or what you will drink; nor about your body, what you will put on. Is not life more than food and the body more than clothing? 26 Look at the birds of the air, for they neither sow nor reap nor gather into barns; yet your heavenly Father feeds them. Are you not of more value than they? ²⁷ Which of you by worrying can add one cubit to his stature?

28 "So why do you worry about clothing? Consider the lilies of the field, how they grow: they neither toil nor spin; ²⁹ and yet I say to you that even Solomon in all his glory was not arrayed like one of these. ³⁰ Now if God so clothes the grass of the field, which today is, and tomorrow is thrown into the oven, will He not much more clothe you, O you of little faith?

31 "Therefore do not worry, saying, 'What shall we eat?' or 'What shall we drink?' or 'What shall we wear?' ³² For after all these things the Gentiles seek. For your heavenly Father knows that you need all these things.

I remember meditating on those verses when I first read them and then thinking, "That is a big promise."

I looked around and thought about how much mankind is driven in pursuit of the needs of life—food, clothing, shelter, and the "big one": approval of others. I added the approval of others because it is such a false narrative that people are driven by. We *are* to be kind to others, but I am talking about trying to impress others through accomplishments or personal success measured in things. In no way am I trying to elevate my accomplishments in this book. I just want to prove what Jesus promised, "Seek first the kingdom of God and His righteousness and all these things shall be added to you."

It took me many years to discover the key phrase in this verse. The phrase that matters the most is, *Seek… His righteousness*. If you seek "His righteousness," the other two statements in the verse happen automatically. His Kingdom *is* righteousness. Seeking and displaying His righteousness is the heart of the Kingdom. I spent many years of my Christian life seeking the Kingdom without seeking His righteousness. Be like Jesus. Study His examples in the Gospels and let the Holy Spirit guide you through every relationship.

Vision and passion are closely related, and they both lead to destiny. For many years, I thought destiny was an end-result that measured success. Then I realized destiny totally belongs to God. I thought destiny was something I would plan out, execute, and then receive a trophy. But God has a divine design. We are to seek that design of His, which forms the destiny of His divine plan. That destiny of God is for us to be with Him and to love Him like He loves us.

This in no way just makes us observers. God's grand design includes our individual design. We are crafted by Him, for Him. He crafts us in such a way that He fulfills the desires he gave us in the beginning. Those desires He planted in us guide us to our destiny, which will be *our* part in His grand design and purpose. The more we grow in this, the more we realize He desires that we partner with Him. We are His workmanship. Not like an employee working for a boss, but rather an ambassador being trained to represent the boss's desires.

Our special talents and gifts are planned by Him. He takes great care in building these talents into our lives. He waits as we learn. When we pledge our lives to Him, He sets up situations that encourage us to choose His perfect way. God is like a father giving advice to a hopeful child. God wants us to lovingly choose to go His way rather than having to be pushed into submission. He is so delighted when we seek His guidance. Then when we obey, God really gets happy. Then when we make it a habit to obey, He rejoices. Then God starts to trust us. It is as if God gets comfortable moving through us.

The main gift or calling God had for me was to be an intercessor. As an intercessor in the church, one's ministry is usually not very visible. Our job is to stand in the gap.

> **Ezek. 22:30** So I sought for a man among them who would make a wall, and stand in the gap before Me on behalf of the land, that I should not destroy it; but I found no one.

The biblical picture we have of Jesus interceding is in Matthew 23:37 "O Jerusalem, Jerusalem, the one who kills the prophets and stones those who are sent to her! How often I wanted to gather your children together, as a hen gathers her chicks under her wings, but you were not willing!

Intercession is when God shares the needs and misdeeds of people and places that do not line up with His Kingdom principles—things that grieve His heart. He then asks you to partner with Him in that grief. According to the scripture in Ezekiel 22, God will consider your prayer toward making a change in that revealed situation. It has a lot to do with not only His training process in our lives but also building intimacy with us.

God told Adam to subdue the earth. Genesis 1:28 Then God blessed them, and God said to them, "Be fruitful and multiply; fill the earth and subdue it; have dominion over the fish of the sea, over the birds of the air, and over every living thing that moves on the earth." (KJV)

This was before man sinned, but the principle remains: We are called on by the Lord to not only take care of the planet but to stand against sin with His righteousness.

Intimacy is so important to the Lord. We must quiet our thoughts so we may hear from Him. I have been visiting houses of prayer since 1996 and I have found it to be the best place to meet with the Lord. The Lord is always with us wherever we are or go but when two or more are gathered in His name, He promises to be in our midst. A house of prayer is a place set aside with an atmosphere suited for seeking that intimacy.

My pastor was given a strong revelation called "In and Out". You come into the presence of the Lord, such as in a house of prayer, to establish that intimacy with Him and then you go out into the world and give Him away. The more I practiced this, the more I found sharing Jesus just became effortless. Jesus did this often. He would go away someplace to spend time with His Father in prayer before doing ministry among people.

This then is the story of my carrying out my destiny, which I came to realize, was God's destiny.

PART ONE

LOST—AND FOUND

Chapter One

I was born in old Saint Paul Hospital in Dallas, Texas, on August 17, 1950. Since then, that building has been demolished and a newer Saint Paul was built just north of downtown Dallas.

The first few years of my life we lived in East Dallas. The first house I remember was located on Santa Fe Street. We moved from there when I was three and moved to the Pleasant Grove area of southwest Dallas.

My father worked for Sherwin-Williams paint manufacturers in East Dallas. I think he had started working there even before he and my mother were married. My mother was a homemaker. I was blessed to always have a mother at home. I started school in Pleasant Grove, at B.H. Macon Elementary. Sometime in the late '50s, Sherwin-Williams moved their factory to Garland, Texas, a suburb northeast of Dallas. In 1960, we moved to a house in Garland on Gary Street. I was in the fifth grade at that time and I went to Caldwell Elementary in Garland.

New school, new friends, new neighbors. The main thing I remember about this change is that the Garland kids were meaner than those in Pleasant Grove. It might have been a false perception because I was the new kid.

While in Pleasant Grove, my sister Glenda was born in 1956. My Grandfather Low had died in 1955 and Grandfather Raulston, on my mother's side, died in 1957. My Grandmother Low had already passed away before I was born, so I never knew her but Grandmother Raulston died in 1988, so I knew her well.

We lived in Garland from 1960 through 1970. There were a lot of kids my age in my neighborhood so that made for lots of fun and trouble. All of us young boys would play street football and other backyard sports. At the end of our street there was a vacant lot owned by the Church of Christ where we would organize larger football games, and boys from other streets would come over. I was never really good at sports, which I feel was because my father was not into sports and he rarely played with me. Plus, shortly after moving to Garland, my father started working the second shift and was not home on the weekday evenings.

I was not a nice, sweet child. I look back and remember I started lying a lot even at eight or nine years old. I began to develop an insecurity problem because of a sense of rejection. I would make up these tall tales to try to impress others, especially the few friends I had. When we moved to Garland, I began to do some petty theft to get things my parents couldn't afford to buy for me—things that other kids had. Then I would lie to my parents, saying I found whatever it was. I remember once I got caught by a store manager when I tried to exit his store with a bar of chocolate hidden in my pocket. He took me to his office and sternly threatened to call my parents if I ever did it again. Although he scared me, I did not change. I guess because I had gotten away with it so many times.

Hebard Sorells was my best friend. He died of cancer in 2017 or 2018, I am not sure. When we were teenagers—about thirteen to sixteen—we liked to sleep out or camp out in the back yard. My father had a pup tent we would use. We would run around the neighborhood during the night. As we got older, we would meet up with friends from other neighborhoods. There was a café that was close by that was open until midnight. By this time, we were slipping around smoking.

Then at age eighteen, Hebard and I started going in different directions. After high school, he went in the military and I started hanging out with hippies. This was the time of the Vietnam War and a draft was imposed on us young men. The draft was set up on a number system and my number was set to come up in the spring of 1970. I had become a full-fledged hippy and all that entailed: smoking dope, dropping LSD, protesting the war, etc. Some of my friends, in order to beat the draft, went to Canada. Canada sympathized and protected those not reporting for the draft and did not extradite them back to the U.S. Another reason was that Canada wanted to boost their population count. Either way, we were in touch with friends up there that could help. So, I was looking into moving to Canada as my draft number got closer.

Then, I got arrested for possession of marijuana. I had two rolled-up marijuana cigarettes and that was a felony crime back in 1970 in Texas. My lawyer indicated that we could beat the case in court if we took it to trial, but a trial would cost more. My family wasn't going to come up with more money, so I had to take a plea-bargain deal with the district attorney. I pleaded guilty to get a two-year probation.

In regards to the draft, I now had a felony case against me and the military would no longer take me. So far as my hippy worldview, I was free from Vietnam and the need to go to Canada. This probation did not affect my lifestyle. I continued to do drugs and was starting to deal drugs. Around the latter part of 1969, a friend had hooked me up with a dealer up in Denton, Texas, who was quite connected with musicians and hippies at North Texas State University. NTSU (now called University of North Texas) was at that time the drop-off place for recreational drugs coming out of the California underground labs and from Mexico.

Before I start another chapter where I talk about my hippy lifestyle, I want to share a few memories of my grandfathers. They both lived within a half mile of each other in the Dimple community north of Clarksville, Texas.

First, about my Grandpa Low. I have only a few memories. I remember once being at his house and as he was sitting in a chair, I got up into his lap and he reached back behind a picture on the wall and pulled out a Jew's harp. He put it to his mouth and began to play. I remember later in life getting my own Jew's harp and my father taught me how to play it.

Also, I remember about a year before my grandfather passed away, he and my step-grandmother Josey came to stay with us. I think he was seeing doctors in Dallas. He would take me for walks and he always had candy in his pocket. Grandpa Charlie Low was a good man. I never heard anything bad about him from the older relatives. They remarked about how he was a godly man. I'm told he died of a blood clot.

Then there was Grandpa Farris Raulston. I remember he had a dog named Bill. Every late afternoon, Bill would be at the front yard gate waiting for my grandpa to drive in from work. Grandpa Raulston worked at the Red River Arsenal near Texarkana. One day, I was at my grandparents' along with my cousin Martha Gail. I called her Gail for short. She and I were having fun throwing things into the property's well. Now this well was their only water source. We even went into the washroom and took the bluing liquid used to whiten clothes and poured it into the well. We were caught and Grandma assured us that Grandpa would deal with us severely when he got home. Gail went into the closet to hide because we thought we were in for a hard whipping. But, when he came home and learned what we had done, I remember Grandpa just sat us down and gave us a serious talk. (Gail and I must have been about five or six years old then.)

Then there was the time Grandpa Raulston took me fishing. We went to a pond somewhere back behind Uncle Clarence's house. Bill, the dog, went with us. I can't remember if we caught anything or not. What I *do* remember was that Grandpa had brought some pieces of liver to use as bait. At one point Grandpa went off into the woods to relieve himself, and while he was gone, Bill ate the liver. Grandpa was so mad that he took the paper the meat was wrapped in and rubbed Bill's nose in it. I was seven years old when Grandpa Raulston died of a heart attack in the middle of the night.

Chapter Two

As history shows, the late Sixties and Seventies saw many changes. We Baby Boomers were coming of age. A big influence on youth was the hippy movement—defined by a lifestyle of rebellion against the cultural norms. We took drugs, we had a "free love" approach to sex, we protested war; we protested everything. We let our hair grow out, etc. There are all kinds of theories as to why this happened, but it was a generation that displayed rebellion and was very irresponsible.

It was the summer of 1968 that I begin to really accept the hippy worldview. I began to smoke marijuana and accept counter-cultural views.

In the fall of 1968, school started back up and I was a senior. Having to go to school five days a week did slow down my drug use. There were even times when I enjoyed school. I had a really interesting English teacher who made literature interesting. At the end of the school year, I was one class short of the credits I needed to graduate with my class. I took a summer class and did get a high school diploma.

I remember when my friend Hebard and I got in trouble at school that senior year. Along with some other students, we tried to lead a student walkout to protest the school rules. This was a time across the nation when many walkouts were being organized. We did not actually have the walkout but the administration suspended us leaders for six weeks. We went to night school in downtown Dallas to make up the classes we were missing.

Funny thing about Hebard—he never wanted to do drugs with me and our relationship slowly drifted apart.

In the summer of 1969, the Texas International Pop Festival happened. This was to be similar to the Woodstock Music Festival in New York. It was set up in a field in Lewisville, north of Dallas. Many of the top rock groups popular at that time appeared there. Of course, I went and stayed high on drugs for three days. I think that at that time I totally sold out to the hippy lifestyle. You might say I swallowed the whole pill.

There was one interesting thing that happened at that Pop Festival. I remember walking out of the festival grounds and seeing a small group of musicians next to a van. The musicians had long hair and were playing music. The van had Bible scriptures written all over it. Then one of them came up and gave me a track. I noticed on the track and on their van was written "Revolutionaries for Christ." I remember standing there wondering, how can this be? How can they have long hair, look like hippies, and be singing about God? I was high at the time, so I put the track in my pocket and left. When I got home, I put the track next to my bed. A few days later, I read it and was still perplexed about these Revolutionaries for Christ. I had encountered my first Jesus Freaks.

I had an aunt who was considered wealthy, according to our family status. Because she had no children, she would help all of her nephews and nieces with college tuition. So, I signed up for some classes for college mainly because of pressure from my extended family. The time came to start college and I was to go to a local college so I could live at home. I went the first day and after class decided this was not for me. I said right then, "I can learn more through doing drugs than going to college."

Just one of many bad decisions in my life.

I had a hard time keeping a steady job and was moving in and out of my parents' house. I would stay out late almost every night. My friends and I would drive around most of the time and meet up at local hangouts. Our town of Garland was "dry," not allowing the sale of alcohol, so there were no bars. Plus, we were mainly doing drugs, not drinking.

It was around the fall of 1969 when I made that connection up in Denton where I could acquire just about any drugs I wanted. Basically, I began to sell drugs to have money and to have drugs to consume myself. I rarely made much money because many people hung around me just to get a free high.

Much of this time my life was in a blur. I was addicted to marijuana. Not being high was a feeling I didn't enjoy. I needed to have my feelings medicated at all times. Even if I did have a job, I had to be able to slip off and smoke a joint so I could stay high on the job.

Now let me explain what was actually happening to me psychologically. My childhood was filled with a growing sense of rejection. I always felt like I did not measure up, or that I was worth less than others. Much of this came from an ongoing rejection from my father. And, I always had a sense that my schoolmates looked down on me. But a funny thing happened when I was doing drugs—now I had friends. This is where the deception came in, because they were only "fair-weather-friends." As long as I had drugs to share, people thought I was cool. As I had access to drugs my popularity would rise. Satan was using the drugs and the people to placate my spirit of rejection.

Looking back, I can't believe some of the stupid things I did back then. I was seriously headed for disaster. One thing I did that ended up sending me to jail and prison was having a party house. I and another young man rented a house north of Garland. This place was in the country and was set up as a party house. It had one big room, a bathroom, kitchen, and out back was a large patio and brick oven.

So, we begin to have parties almost every night. Loud music and drugs were flowing. Here I am on probation and I am shining a spotlight on me as bright as can be. Sure enough, one night that fall I came home to find the house surrounded by cars. I even noticed one of the cars that looked like a car I knew a narcotic agent drove. But I dismissed that thought and went on in the front door. There, to my surprise, were the police, narcotic agents, and my friends sitting on the floor with guns pointed at them. They told me I was under arrest along with everyone else.

They said they found marijuana in a shirt pocket in the closet. Weeks before this I had been feeling really paranoid and had been demanding that no one do drugs in the house or even carry drugs into the house. I had been warned by some friends that the house was being watched. It ended up that everyone was let go except for my roommate and me. Both of us were on probation so we could not bail out of jail.

Overall, this was a rotten deal. In the trial that followed it came down to determining whose shirt pocket was it in? The police did not keep the shirt to present it in court. We had a joint trial, and it was looking good for us because the police could not prove whose shirt they had found the marijuana in. The prosecution asked for a postponement until the next day. That night they went out and arrested a collaborating witness. A young lady had stayed with us for a week or so. The next day of the trial she was brought into the court. She was dressed up in a cute dress and a bow in her hair. As far as we knew, she had been set up with immunity to testify against us. She was put on the witness stand, projected to be a picture of innocence, and began to tell of all the wild parties we had. My lawyer and my roommate's lawyer did not do a good job of interrogating this young lady. The jury convicted us of possession of marijuana. It was obvious the ownership of the marijuana could not be established but the lady's testimony swayed the jury. The very fact that we were both on probation for drug offenses is what took us down.

Chapter Three

I was in the Dallas County jail awaiting trial. Because of being on probation, I was not allowed to get out on bail. After about a month, my mother came to visit me. She asked me what I needed and I told her of a few things. I also told her that we could receive books. She said, "Remember that Bible I gave you when you graduated from high school? I will have them bring it to you."

"Sure," I said.

A few days later she brought the Bible and it was brought to me in the cell block. I had noticed a few other guys there reading Bibles, so I thought to myself, *this isn't going to look weird.*

Now, my mother had taken me to church and Sunday school all throughout my young life. So, I knew about Jesus and many of the stories in the Bible. The thought went through my mind, *Why not take this time to read the Bible all the way through.*

Well, of course, there is the Old Testament and the New Testament, and although the Old Testament comes first, I said to myself, *I think I will read the New Testament first.*

Now, you need to realize my present state of mind. I was a hippy. One thing hippies thought about often was all the injustices in the world. We believed in peace, not war. We believed the world was being run by greedy men. Since everything is stacked against you, you might as well just be free.

To my surprise, as I began to read the New Testament, I saw Jesus as a hippy in His day. He was no doubt doing good and the rulers of His day were against Him. He came up against the establishment and their traditions. He even protested at the Temple. The more I read of the New Testament—the books of Matthew, Mark and Luke—I was starting to get mad. As I read the sayings of Jesus, I realized these were amazing truths He was laying out. I was mad because He said these things two thousand years ago so why haven't men learned by now.

Then I started reading the book of John. I got to the third chapter and began to read about Nicodemus coming to question Jesus.

3:1 There was a man of the Pharisees named Nicodemus, a ruler of the Jews. ² This man came to Jesus by night and said to Him, "Rabbi, we know that You are a teacher come from God; for no one can do these signs that You do unless God is with him."

3 Jesus answered and said to him, "Most assuredly, I say to you, unless one is born again, he cannot see the kingdom of God."

4 Nicodemus said to Him, "How can a man be born when he is old? Can he enter a second time into his mother's womb and be born?"

5 Jesus answered, "Most assuredly, I say to you, unless one is born of water and the Spirit, he cannot enter the kingdom of God. ⁶ That which is born of the flesh is flesh, and that which is born of the Spirit is spirit. ..."

Upon reading that, something clicked in my heart. "That's it! That is what I need. I need to be born of the Spirit."

So, right there in a Dallas County jail cell, I asked Jesus to come into my heart. This was December 17, 1970. Not only was there a peace that came over me but the word SATISFACTION in big letters kept scrolling across my mind. This was such a deep experience that I have never doubted I was "born again."

SATISFACTION in big letters kept scrolling across my mind. This was such a deep experience that I have never doubted I was "born again."

I got such a hunger to read the Bible I would sit on my cell-bunk and read for hours and hours. Although I went to Bible school years later, this time in the Dallas County jail was where I really learned many valuable truths. During this time, I encountered many cults and eastern philosophies. We inmates would discuss religion for hours. I had to really watch myself because some were believable even when they had twisted scripture references. There was one man that was determined to turn me into a Jehovah's Witness. In a way, he helped me a lot because I knew he was wrong, and I searched the scriptures to prove him wrong.

There was also a man who had written material from The Children of God. This was a fringe group of Jesus Freaks, who had some radical beliefs. They took Acts 4: 32-35 to be a present-day command.

> **32** Now the multitude of those who believed were of one heart and one soul; neither did anyone say that any of the things he possessed was his own, but they had all things in common. 33 And with great power the apostles gave witness to the resurrection of the Lord Jesus. And great grace was upon them all. 34 Nor was there anyone among them who lacked; for all who were possessors of lands or houses sold them, and brought the proceeds of the things that were sold, 35 and laid them at the apostles' feet; and they distributed to each as anyone had need.

They believed that when you gave your life to Jesus then you gave up everything and separated yourself into a community where everyone had everything in common. I became very favorable to this group. They had a way of mixing the hippy lifestyle with biblical principles. Later on, once I was out of prison, I visited a few of their communes where they all lived together.

I do thank the Lord that He protected me from being part of The Children of God. As years went on, they really fell into false doctrine by following a false prophet.

To end this chapter, I went to trial and received a two-year prison sentence. I went down to the Texas Penitentiary to serve out the remainder of my time. I was locked up for one-and-a-half years.

In the penitentiary, I was on the Ferguson Farm. At that time, Ferguson was mainly for first offenders but they worked us hard.

One verse that really caught my attention at that time was:

Romans 14:8 For whether we live, we live unto the Lord; and whether we die, we die unto the Lord: whether we live therefore, or die, we are the Lord's.

I did not know how much I would be tested along the lines of that verse in my next season. Having been released from prison in the spring of 1972, I went to live with my uncle and aunt in Oklahoma. My uncle owned a heavy equipment business and I worked around the machinery doing odd jobs.

Chapter Four

Now when I got out of prison I was determined to live for Jesus. I was baptized and gave my testimony to some youth groups. The church that my uncle, aunt and cousins attended had a few young people my age. The pastor saw me as having a good influence on them, but when I began to run around with these young people outside of church, I began to get fleshly. I was older, so they looked up to me. Generally, they liked to drink alcohol and hang out at small town bars. I began to let myself just go along with them. Since I was not upholding my Christian testimony, I ended up introducing these young people to drugs. There is a scripture that describes this time in my life:

> **Proverbs 26:11** As a dog returns to his own vomit, So a fool repeats his folly.

There was also another thing the devil did that had induced these young people to go back to alcohol. The pastor I mentioned above, and his wife, were truly a good influence on the young people in the area.

Now I will tell this story as it was told to me. I do not know if it is the complete truth or not. The bars in the area were owned or financed by some of the church members. With these young people getting saved and no longer hanging out at the bars, money was now being lost. So, some of these members stirred up others against the pastor and his wife. A meeting for a vote of confidence was called for the church members to attend. The church was packed. Many of the people from the community that I had never seen in the church attended. They had the vote, and the pastor was voted out. Before leaving, he admonished me to carry on, but I had been embittered, along with all the young people. The devil had won and I was of no help. I was basically a new Christian and at this time had not been baptized by fire.

One night I was in one of the bars meeting with someone. The parents of one of these young people that had been attending the church came up to my table and confronted me. They basically told me to get out of Oklahoma or my life would be in danger. They had already talked to my uncle and aunt, and my parents in Texas had been asked to come pick me up.

Another tragic thing occurred at this time. My father was not a Christian. He personally stated that he believed I had not truly become a Christian but had made a false confession to get out of trouble. This went really deep. Did I help my father once again turn away from salvation? In 2006, my father died of Alzheimer's without making a public confession of faith. I thank the Lord for forgiving me, but it is something that really sobers me.

After being run out of Oklahoma (as I like to dramatically put it), I stopped doing drugs for a while. I got back to Garland and found out many of my former drug buddies had become Christians. The Holy Spirit was being poured out through the Jesus movement in the early '70s. I began to connect with these brothers and sisters and became really encouraged.

Now, we were real Jesus Freaks. We brought our hippy lifestyle right over into our Jesus experience. We had long hair, cared less about how we looked, and just didn't try to fit in. We especially did not fit at church. Traditional churches did not want us until we cleaned up. There were a few churches across the country that were reaching out to the Jesus Freaks, but not many. Mostly we would meet as small groups in homes. Some were living together in communal houses somewhat like the hippy "crash pads" we had become accustomed to. God was doing amazing things to set people free of drugs and all kinds of demons. We were radical for Jesus, witnessing to everyone, and carrying our Bibles in our hands everywhere we went. People were getting baptized in water, Holy Spirit and fire.

I remember it was a time where I began to be tossed back and forth between my flesh and my spirit. I had not been baptized in fire yet, so I was straddling the fence still. In this time of tossing, sometimes I would contact some of my former drug buddies that were still doing drugs and go out with them to get high. Then I would feel bad about having gotten high and would contact my Christian friends. I was back and forth between these two groups of friends for about a year. By the summer of 1974, I had so turned back to drugs that I had become a serious drug dealer.

A strange thing happened: though I was doing drugs, I was not really getting any thrills from it. It was like I knew I was doing wrong but I just could not seem to stop. Later, I realized the devil had that old rejection hook in my soul. The fact that people would come to me for drugs fed my ego.

One scary situation that happened at this time I knew was a warning from God. I was riding around with three other friends and we were high on drugs. They were laughing about something and suddenly their heads turned reptilian. It was only for an instant, but I could see the demons that were possessing them. Still, even after this, I did not turn back to the Lord.

The Lord was working out a plan to redeem me. There was an undercover narcotic agent who befriended me and started buying drugs from me. He came flashing money at me and had a story that he was buying so he could resell them up north.

One night I had set it up for him to buy $10,000 worth of clinical THC (the equivalent of $55,000 today). I rode with him to Arlington, Texas, where we were to make the transaction. This was happening at a friend's house. We arrived and parked. Before going in, the undercover agent showed me the money and said he would stick it under the front seat and once we examined the drugs he would come out to get the money. So, we went into the house. Now, my friend was running a business out of his house and there were a number of people there. The man who was to deliver the THC had not arrived yet. So, we waited. Finally, the man arrived and the agent examined the product. Like he planned, he went out to get the money. All of a sudden, police started coming through every door (often I joke that I think one even came down the chimney). The police started putting handcuffs on us and announcing we were under arrest.

Just then, something profound happened to me. As the undercover agent was putting the cuffs on me and was reading off the indictments against me, a PEACE came over me. I said to myself, *I encountered the Lord in Jail, and He is still going to be there.*

See, all this time while I was doing drugs, even selling drugs, I was miserable. When they took us to the Arlington city jail and were interrogating me, I was totally oblivious of my severe situation. They were saying, "Don't you know how much trouble you are in, six felonies of drug sales? We are going to put you in jail for the rest of your life."

All I could think about was the peace I felt. As I look back on that day, I realize that is the day Jesus baptized me with fire. (Matthew 3:11) From then until now, I have been sold out to God.

Yes, I experienced being baptized in fire, but I still had a lot of junk in my life. For about six months, I was in the Tarrant County jail in Fort Worth, Texas. The bail bond to get out of jail was so high that there was no way I or my family could pay it. I think my family had the attitude that jail was the best place for me since every time I had gotten out I did not seem to change. Looking back, I am really convinced being in jail with my Bible was God's best plan for me.

For about half that time I was in a cell block with roughly thirty other prisoners. A few notable things happened while I was in that jail.

First, one day in the cell block we were karate-chopping wooden dominoes. Let me see if I can explain this. We were taking two dominoes, standing them up and then laying another domino across those two standing. Then we would karate-chop the domino lying flat, breaking that domino. So, when it was my turn somehow I hit it wrong and the bone in my hand broke. The guard was called and they took me to the hospital (in chains). They thought I was lying to them about the dominoes. They thought I had been in a fight. When they brought me back to the jail they did not put me in a cell block with the other prisoners. I was confined to isolation instead. This is one of those cells for the real troublemakers. I now had a cast on my right arm so I realized they did not want me clobbering someone with the cast. After a day or so, I thought, *This is cool, a room of my own.*

While in isolation, I can't remember how but I got the book *Tortured for Christ* by Richard Wurmbrand. Richard Wurmbrand was a pastor during the brutal reign of communism in Romania. He was imprisoned and tortured for over fourteen years. His book really opened my eyes to the persecuted life Christians had to live in the communist, atheist countries of the Soviet bloc. I thought to myself, *Here he is in jail for doing good, but I am in jail for doing bad.* Somehow there was a connection made in my heart where I became very empathetic toward people living under communist rule. I wanted to know all I could about communism and the persecuted Christians. Little did I know that at that time God was setting forth my destiny. I began to pray and intercede for the communist world. I felt that God wanted me to develop a passion for intercession.

After the cast was taken off my hand, I still remained in isolation for several months until they put me back in a cell block with other prisoners. One Sunday, a man came to the outside of the bars and began to speak to us prisoners about Jesus. Most of the prisoners paid him very little attention but I was really interested and admired the boldness he had. He handed me a magazine from Christ for the Nations (CFNI). I had heard of CFNI before from one of my friends who had become a Christian. I took the magazine and read it cover to cover. I wrote to CFNI and asked for a subscription to be mailed to me. For the rest of the time in jail and prison, I received the monthly magazine.

I went to court on a case in Tarrant County for sales of a controlled substance and received my sentence. I was given three years in prison, but now I would have to be transferred to the Dallas County Jail to face more drug charges there. Once in the Dallas County Jail, I went into a strange, defensive mode.

Like I mentioned before, I was just a poor prisoner. I had to depend on the state to appoint a lawyer to represent me in court. Of course, my court-appointed lawyer didn't even try to fight my case for me, so I had to do what I could to fight for myself. Even before I was taken to Dallas County, I had started working on my cases. They were the most serious ones, and those were the cases where they really planned to put me away for the rest of my life. When I finally met my court-appointed lawyer in Dallas, I realized he was not going to help me at all.

It was so crazy, but in the cell block that I landed in, there were what we call "jailhouse lawyers." These were guys like me, poor and having to depend on court-appointed lawyers. Now the good thing was that new rulings had been passed in Texas that prisoners could not be denied law books and material. So, I became a jailhouse lawyer myself, or at least I helped these guys that were navigating the legal system. We were writing writs of habeas corpus and discovery, forcing the courts to comply with legal statutes. We even saw some people get released from jail because of our writs.

I needed the formal copies of the indictments of cases charged against me. So, I sent a letter of request to the Dallas Sheriff Department and I was denied those formal copies. We did the research in the laws and found that the Sheriff Department was in violation. If I remember right, I appealed to the Dallas County Court to force them to provide those indictments. The Dallas County Court did not comply. My next step was to appeal to the federal court. In order to appeal to the federal court, I needed to file a lawsuit against the Dallas County Sheriff Department. So, I took that step and filed the suit with the federal court in Dallas. The federal court in Dallas denied the suit.

I did not give up. I went on and appealed my case to the Fifth Circuit Court of Appeals in New Orleans. I was amazed when the district court accepted my appeal, saying it had merit. They had put it on their docket, but had not set a date. So here I had a $35,000 lawsuit against the Dallas Sheriff Department, and I was in jail facing a district attorney's office that wanted to give me many years in jail. By the way, my court-appointed lawyer had informed me that if I took my case to court, the district attorney was asking the court to give me thirty years.

It was a known fact that cases like mine, being brought before the federal District Court of Appeals, were subject to a seven-year wait. So, here was my reasoning: I would force the county to try all my cases against me, hoping for one of two outcomes—they would reason it to be too burdensome and drop the cases, which would mean I would just serve the time for the Tarrant County offense I had pleaded guilty to, or I would end up with a large sentence like the District Attorney wanted, hoping that it would get overturned by my federal lawsuit. As the years passed, I could increase the lawsuit to an even larger amount. Therefore, there was a hope I would get out in seven years and have money to live on.

Let me stop here and point out something. Men live on hope. Hope is built into us by God, or we would be subject to deep depression, even suicide. Even people in jail have hope of a better outcome.

Working through my court-appointed lawyer, the court date was set for me to go to trial. I had all but lost hope that they would drop the Dallas cases and just let me do the Tarrant County time, which was three years.

You have to realize at this point I was still studying my Bible and trying to be a Christian in jail. I felt that these court proceedings were just me pursuing my rights. Most people would think, *just own up to the fact that you did wrong and take your time.* Well…the day before I was to go to court the Lord spoke to me. I was reading in 1 Corinthians 6: 6 But brother goes to law against brother, and that before unbelievers! 7 Now therefore, it is already an utter failure for you that you go to law against one another. Why do you not rather accept wrong? Why do you not rather let yourselves be cheated?

The Lord clearly spoke through this verse the words "Why do you not rather accept wrong? Why do you not let yourselves be cheated?"

See, I was so tied up in my defensive attitude that I was going to great lengths to beat the authorities. The Lord spoke to me and said, "Okay, maybe you are being cheated by the Sheriff's department, but hey, you know you sold those drugs to that undercover agent and you are guilty of that. Why not accept the fact that you are being wronged in a small way and just accept the sentence given you."

The next morning, I met my court-appointed lawyer in court with a totally new plan. He was shocked, but relieved. I told him I wanted to suspend the trial and plead guilty. I would then drop the lawsuit against the Sheriff's department and let the judge sentence me. Whatever the judge gave me I would live with. He went through the motions before the court and I threw myself on the mercies of the judge. Now remember, my lawyer had already told me the district attorney wanted a thirty-year sentence. This was where I was just going to have to trust God to speak to the judge. So, when the judge said six years I was shocked. From a possible thirty to six. Wow! God's mercy is so amazing.

By now, I had been locked up for about one and one-half years. So, I was looking at a maximum of four and one-half more. Now here is where another blessing comes into effect. In the Texas Penitentiary, if you do not cause any trouble, you can earn "Good time." This can be up to two days for every one you serve. Every day of my sentence would count as two against the overall sentence. This meant that the six years could actually be three years. And, when you are sentenced in Texas, the time you spent in local jails waiting to go to court counts as time served. I had already done one-and-a-half years and I could be getting out in one-and-a-half more.

Chapter Five

The first time I went to prison I was on the Ferguson Unit. I worked in the fields for the first half of the time I was there and the other half I got into a small engine-repair class. It was hard labor out in those fields. The field bosses would drive us hard. I nearly collapsed a number of times.

The second time in the Texas prison I was assigned to the Tag Plant on the Winn Unit, where the auto license plates are made. One thing about the Texas prison—you had to work. I was given the job of quality control. When the plate came out of the oven, they were put into stacks of fifty. I would take a stack and go through it one by one to make sure the ink was not smeared or misprinted. If I found one or more misprinted, then I would have to walk it through the process of having it remade. I would have to take that tag from station to station until it was put back into the oven. That means I got to walk through the whole tag plant visiting with many of the men.

In prison, we could order Christian books and materials to be sent in to us. At that time, these Chick Publication Christian cartoon booklets were popular. They were a great tool for witnessing Christian truths. They fit conveniently in my pocket. I would take these with me to the Tag Plant and would give them to the guys at each station to read. After one guy read one, I would pick it up from him on my next round and take it to the next guy until it had been read at each station. This was my way of evangelizing in prison.

While there in the Winn Unit, I encountered some other guys that were burning for the Lord. We had a group and we would meet every chance we got. There was a Chapel that met every Sunday and we would meet there. There were many different denominations in the prison and each one was allowed to have their own Sunday School class.

Now the chaplain did not like Pentecostals. Our Sunday school class was actually a Baptist class at first, but some of us were "spirit-filled," so we went to the chaplain and asked for a Pentecostal/Charismatic class. He denied us the class and even made rude remarks about such a thing. Okay, so here is where the jailhouse lawyers went into action. The first step was to write a letter to the main warden over the whole prison system. The letter informed him that our religious rights were being violated and unless there was a remedy we would file a religious discrimination lawsuit against the prison system.

I was told that the warden made a special trip to the chaplain's office to scold him into giving us our class because they did not need a religious discrimination lawsuit. Actually, the Baptist Sunday School class became the Pentecostal class because the man leading it had been spirit-filled.

Before the warden had made his visit, we had another problem. Each time we had our Sunday School class, there would be a time of hymns, and then the chaplain would give a sermon. Basically, it was like a traditional church service. Now we Pentecostals would be getting blessed during the hymn time and we would raise our hands. The chaplain would instruct the guards to remove us from the service. He was a hard-core Methodist and did not like charismatics.

Like I said above, we would meet every chance we could get. One of the places we would meet was out on the yard. "Out on the yard" was time given once or twice a week to go outside onto the big field within the high fences. On the field, we could organize games, walk around, or exercise. We charismatics would circle up, sitting on the field, and pray and talk about Jesus. Other prisoners would make fun of us, sometimes throwing rocks at us. Some of the guards would even encourage these troublemakers.

Another place we would get together was the law library. In Texas prisons it was mandated by federal law that prisoners had to have access to law books so they could research and prepare legal documents. We charismatics would meet there, check out law books, lay the books in front of us, and then talk about Jesus.

One of the charismatic Christians was quite well-off financially. He was ordering Christian books all the time. He would make these books available to the rest of us too.

In prison, of course, you can't just go and come anytime you want. But there were other places we could briefly connect—the cafeteria, the regular prison library, etc. Almost every time we would meet up, we would be passing books back and forth.

We were just hungry for God. We would witness to other prisoners and we saw some get saved. Our Pentecostal class grew and grew. We began to see the gifts of the Spirit manifest when we would meet up, especially in the Sunday School class.

Of all the many lessons I learned in prison, the second time gave me the lesson to be honoring and respectful of others, even if they are perceived as my enemy.

Once when I was coming back from the chow hall and walking down the long corridor to my cell block, I was taking my time, stopping to look out the windows. Down at the cell block entrance, the guard was waiting to open the block door for me. I wasn't even thinking about him when he hollered at me, "Hey, you, I am waiting on your sorry ass. Hurry up you sorry ol' thing."

I'm not sure those were his exact words, but he was mad. I know he was expecting me to say something disrespectful to him. That was just how the general relationship between guards and prisoners was. God spoke to me and said, "Be respectful." So, when I approached him, I said, "Sir, I am so sorry."

I'll never forget the look on his face. He did not know how to respond. He was surprised by a prisoner being respectful toward him. God used that situation to prove the scripture to me, Matthew 5:25

Agree with your adversary quickly, while you are on the way with him, lest your adversary deliver you to the judge, the judge hand you over to the officer, and you be thrown into prison.

Well, I was already in prison so maybe the second half of the verse does not apply. (Over the years I have seen this played out. At times I would be pulled over for traffic violations and by being respectful and admitting my guilt, I would only be given a warning.)

While I was in prison this time, there was a verse that became my favorite verse in the Bible. Isaiah 55:12 –

> For you shall go out with joy,
> And be led out with peace;
> The mountains and the hills
> Shall break forth into singing before you,
> And all the trees of the field shall clap their hands.

In prison you have every demon that can be thought of. But when I quoted and meditated on this verse, I could walk through the prison knowing I was beloved and forgiven by the Lord. I would imagine the red brick walls and the green bars celebrating that a child of God was walking by. Even today, I enjoy the liberating assurance this verse gives.

Chapter Six

Finally, a few months short of three years, I was released from prison on parole.

Beverly Hills Baptist Church was a Charismatic church in Dallas that I had connected with while I was in the Dallas county jail. I had visited there once in my Jesus Freak days, but since it was on the other side of town I only went that one time. It was one of the few churches reaching out to the hippies in the early Seventies. I remember a group of us had visited and I was amazed to see so many hippies in the congregation.

While I was in the Dallas county jail in 1975, I had sent a letter to the church and they sent a minister to meet me in the jail. Brother Louie was the pastor of their prison ministry and we had stayed in contact while I was in prison. The church started a "halfway house" called the Jericho Home. It was for ex-drug addicts, men coming out of prison, and those just needing discipline. The rules were strict: you had to stay in the house or on the property, no walking off. We all came and went together. Limited visits were allowed from family and we had Bible classes almost every day. We attended Beverly Hills and had the job of cleaning the church after services. When I came out of prison, I submitted myself to the Jericho Home.

I found out that Christ for the Nations (CFNI) was having their graduation ceremony one Sunday afternoon. This was May or June 1977. I got permission for us at the Jericho Home to go. This was a monumental visit for me. The service began with worship. When the worship started, many of the students began to dance. I was amazed. At Beverly Hills, I had seen people dance at times, but something was different at CFNI. There was a level of freedom I had never seen before. My spirit-man was jumping for joy. I asked the Lord if I could go to the school. Then a sequence of events happened, and I moved on campus for the fall session of 1977.

One notable thing that happened was that I had contacted Texas Rehabilitation Commission. Their representative met with me and said he would try to help me by applying for funds for me to go to CFNI. He told me he had never tried to get a grant for a Bible school before and was not sure it could be done. But thanks be to God, I got the support. I had no idea how much my life was to change.

All my time in jail and prison for the past three years I had been studying the Bible. I had a lot of knowledge of the Bible, but I had little spiritual transformation in my life. Now at CFNI, worship and prayer were the atmosphere. It was like you were in school with the Holy Spirit. The best way I can describe what was happening to me for the next two years is that the Holy Spirit was cleaning me out. Most of that came through tears of repentance. I soaked the carpet at CFNI with my tears. There was so much junk in my life that had to go.

One of the requirements at CFNI was to be part of an outreach ministry. So, I joined the jail ministry. We would go to the Dallas County Jail and preach/speak to the prisoners about Jesus. This was amazing. We saw many give their lives to Jesus. I realized something—jail ministry is the easiest ministry of all. In jail a person is at a crisis point in their life and they can better realize their need for a Savior. I ended up leading the group.

At this time I was still going to Beverly Hills Baptist Church and involved in the prison ministry there. We would go to Texas State and federal prisons and preach. Often, I would share my testimony and see people come to Jesus.

Also, at CFNI I would meet with the Underground Church prayer group. We would pray for Christians suffering for Jesus in communist lands. Remember, when I was in Tarrant County Jail, God had really touched my heart for these dear saints.

There was a young lady I had become friends with who also had a burden for communist countries. While everyone else was having coffee, Cokes and donuts during the break between classes, Leslie and I would meet in the prayer room to pray. Usually, we would be there twice a week and would pray for a different communist country each time. We became good friends and did some dating. We kissed a few times, but we tried our best to keep it on a spiritual level. Of course, there were times I thought she was the one. Then she began to get a burden for China, but I was more inclined toward Eastern Europe. We began to see God was directing us in different directions, so we stopped dating. I was somewhat brokenhearted but years later I realized that God was saving me from making a wrong choice.

There was a habit I was really having trouble getting rid of, and that was smoking. I had to have a cigarette every three or four hours. Smoking was definitely not allowed on campus at Christ for the Nations, so I would sneak around to smoke and eat mints to cover it up. Several years passed before I was free from smoking, but you will read about that later on in the book.

After my first semester at CFNI, I moved off campus into a nearby apartment with another roommate. He was not a student at CFNI but we were friends at church. He also went through the Jericho Home at Beverly Hills.

Then a friend at CFNI, I'll call her Christine, approached me one day and introduced me to a young man who needed a place to stay. I'm not sure how she met him. He was not a student at CFNI. He was considering going when the next semester started. So, Jeff moved in with Don and me. This started a new friendship that lasted many years. Although he ended up not going to CFNI after all, he was a kind, moral man who had a good influence on me.

Christine brought over another friend, Karen, who also needed a place to stay. Karen was from Iowa and her male friend also came from Iowa. Hey, we welcomed him because he reduced the rent to be shared among four guys. Before we knew it, this new guy had other friends that showed up from Iowa. I think all together three more moved in with us. We were now eight people living in a two-bedroom apartment. Gradually, they all found jobs and moved out. One of the guys from Iowa had a sister who joined us. Later on, Don, my first roommate, married her.

During this time of many roommates, I realized something: I was having a conflict with secular forces that was hindering my spiritual life. These guys where confessing Christians, but their maturity level was shallow. I realized I needed to do something to keep from slipping backwards spiritually. I asked God to help me find better friends. I loved to pray and do street witnessing. So, I looked for prayer and outreach groups.

I graduated from Christ for the Nations and I also changed churches. Beverly Hills had become a really big church. They were the largest church in Dallas with about four thousand attending every Sunday. They were having to meet in a rented auditorium. Let me give a brief history. Beverly Hills' pastor, Howard Canaster, received the baptism of the Holy Spirit and did not fit the Baptist mold any longer. Although Beverly Hills was growing by leaps and bounds, the Southern Baptism association of Dallas decided to dis-fellowship them from the association.

· · · · · ·

SHADY GROVE – A NEW BEGINNING

Another Baptist church in the association that was dis-fellowshipped was Shady Grove Baptist Church in Grand Prairie. One day the pastor from Shady Grove came and preached at Beverly Hills. I just really liked this guest pastor. His name was Olen Griffing. While I was still at CFNI, Olen came and spoke there once and because the girl I was dating at CFNI was attending Shady Grove, I went with her one time.

When it was about time for me to graduate, I decided to start going to Shady Grove.

There were many reasons I changed churches. First, Leslie, my former girlfriend, attended there, and I still had a hope we would get back together. She soon went back to Minnesota but I stayed. Second, that Sunday in June of 1979 when I went to check out the church, God clearly spoke to me that He wanted me at Shady Grove. During the service, a man got up and confessed a sin he was involved in, in front of the church. This amazed me; I knew we were to confess our sins to one another, but I had never seen this before. Also, one of my teachers at CFNI had said something really powerful during class one day. He said we needed to be sure to get established in a church once we graduated. I was feeling lost in the big Beverly Hills Church and knew I wanted to be in a smaller church. All these factors entered into my decision. I had determined that the next Sunday, I was going to join Shady Grove. I told one of my Iowa friends about the church and he came with me that next Sunday.

Now this was back when Shady Grove was still a Baptist church. At the end of the service, my friend and I came forward to join the church. The procedure was that if you wanted to become a member then at the end of the service you would come to the front, tell the pastor you wanted to become a member, and then you filled out an information card. So that is how I joined Shady Grove Baptist Church. Later, the church dropped the Baptist name.

That particular Sunday, something special was happening: a couple was getting married at the end of the service. Mike and Allana had both graduated from Wycliff Bible Translators and wanted to get married before going to Malaysia as missionaries. Pastor Olen asked them to come forward. Mike and Allana were not originally from the Dallas area so there was no one from their families there, so Pastor Olen then turned to my friend from Iowa and me, asking us to stand in as the wedding party. The wedding took place, and we were the witnesses standing in for the wedding of a couple that went on to give a remote people group in Malaysia a written language.

God was moving at Shady Grove Church and you never knew what would happen on a Sunday morning or at that time even in the evening service. I never wanted to miss a service, just because you did not want to miss God when He showed up. And He always showed up.

Chapter Seven

As I mentioned, I was always looking for new friends. I loved to pray with others, so if I heard of a prayer group meeting, I would try to attend. I also would organize prayer groups and get involved with groups that were doing street witnessing. We would target events like rock concerts and witness in front of the venue. We saw some people get saved but mainly we were ignored. We were just passionate about witnessing.

I think it was about 1981 when the Rolling Stones were doing a tour of the United States. They had two concerts planned for Dallas. They were to appear in the Cotton Bowl for two nights. At this time, before it was remodeled, it would seat about fifty- to sixty thousand. Their concerts were highly promoted. There were t-shirts printed up for all the U.S venues with the words Sold Out written across it.

A few of us started to pray about this coming concert. We felt we were called to go witness at the concert so we asked the Lord for a strategy. I took the task of putting together a special handout that we would hand out outside the building after the concert. I did some research on the Rolling Stones and found satanic influences—not only in the words of their songs but in the logos and the band's history. I wrote up a three-fold handout that resembled an information brochure. We had three thousand printed up and decided to hand these out after the concert as people were coming out.

The day before the first night of the concert people were already camping out in front of the Cotton Bowl. A friend of mine and I decided to go and do a prayer walk around the venue. We prayer-walked around the Cotton Bowl and ended up on the front steps where people were camped out. We got on our knees and just prayed our hearts out. People were making fun of us and throwing things at us.

Then, the first night of the concert, we had a team ready to hand out the brochures. At the bottom of the brochure was an appeal for salvation and a phone number they could call. So, as people were exiting the event we passed out all three thousand and people were eager to have it. I had passed out gospel tracts before at concerts and would see many of them just thrown on the ground. This was different—few were found thrown away.

My phone number was on the brochure. I can't remember the roommates I was living with at that time, but we were ready to answer the phone if it rang. Over the next few days we had twelve calls and three accepted the Lord over the phone. So, we felt God had used us for those three.

There were also two other things that happened that showed God's hand. The Dallas events did not sell out for the Rolling Stones. Also, on the second night, a fierce storm came over the Cotton Bowl and everyone got soaked. In the newspaper the next day was a picture of Mick Jagger pointing his finger into the air and demanding the storm to stop. It did not stop and the thunder roared even more.

About this same time, I started mailing Bible portions into Russia. The ministry Voice of the Martyrs, founded by Richard Wurmbrand, would send out packets that contained portions of the Bible in Russian, along with addresses of families in large cities in the Soviet Union. You would write the address on the envelope, take it to the post office, and pay for mailing it airmail. The ministry had copies of telephone books from these cities so they could get the names and addresses. Most were actually going to nonbelievers because few Christians were allowed a telephone. They said that through all the partners in the West over time they would try to get the whole Bible to each address. I was so glad to participate in this type of outreach.

I also got involved with the abortion issue. I joined a group of ladies that did what was called "sidewalk counseling." They would stand in front of abortion providers' buildings and try to intercept women coming in for abortions. We would try and talk them into keeping their unborn baby. I think I was mainly there to protect the ladies that were actually doing the counseling.

One time, I had to confront a father who was really aggressive, but God intervened. Another instance was when I approached a man who was waiting in his car after his girlfriend had entered the abortion clinic. I gave him our literature and asked him to read it while he was waiting. Then I joined the ladies on the sidewalk. A few minutes later, the young man got out of his car, went into the clinic, and brought his girlfriend out. He brought her over to us and told her to talk to us. Many babies were saved through this method of sidewalk counseling. At this time, our group did not have a program for extended care for the rescued mothers or babies. I was so glad to see these kinds of programs set up in later years.

Let me share a short story that happened about this time in my life.

My roommate Don wanted to go visit his parents in northern Arkansas. So, I decided to go with him. Don had an older Volkswagen Bug. We took off for Arkansas, which was about a complete day trip. His parents were happy to see us. I had a separate side trip I wanted to take while en route. I had heard of a Christian commune in Southern Missouri that I wanted to visit. My problem was that I did not have an address. I knew the name of the place and that it was just outside the town of Branson. So, we decide to go look for it. We thought we would go and ask around in the town.

In the later '80s, a lot of investment went into Branson and it became a vacation hot spot. But this was around 1980 or '81 and Branson was mainly undeveloped. By the time we got to Branson, it was already past sunset. So, we started asking around town to get some directions. Most of the people did not know what we were talking about. Finally, we talked to someone who somewhat helped us. He told us of a group of young people who lived together up a road not far out of town. This sounded promising so we took off to find them. We found the dirt road we had been directed to and noticed a sign with an arrow pointing up the road. The sign said "The Zone." Well, that is not the name we were looking for, but we went up the road anyway. It took us to an old house. It was a big house so it could be possible that many people lived there.

By now the sun had been down for a few hours. We got out of the car and went to the front door. We knocked and someone opened the door. They just motioned for us to come in. We walked in and immediately noticed marijuana smoke. There were many young people sitting around and rock music was playing. We immediately realized we had stumbled onto something we were not expecting. I remember these people just staring at us, stoned out of their minds and wondering who we might be.

We explained that we were looking for a Christian commune. Of course, they said that was not them, which we'd already figured out. So, Don and I left and counted this side trip as a failure.

I cannot remember how many days we were there at his parents' but Sunday morning we started back to Texas. Both of us needed to be back at work the next day.

Now Don's Volkswagen was not in the best shape. We realized we were demanding a lot from it on this trip. So, we were on our way back home and just on the other side of Little Rock, Arkansas, the car just totally broke down. Here we were, stranded and with very little money between us. We sat there trying to figure out what to do. We knew we needed to get back to Texas that day. We decided to call his father and he agreed to come pick up the car the next day. The only thing for us to do was hitchhike to Dallas. So that is what we did.

We were on the side of the highway with our thumbs out. I can't remember how long it was but here came an old bus. The bus was going slow, so I told Don, "I think they are going to pick us up." When they passed us, as they were coming to a stop, we noticed written on the side of the bus, in big letters, was The Revelation Singers. So, we were happy, thinking some Christians were picking us up.

The door swung open and a long-haired bearded man at the wheel greeted us and told us to get in. We got in. He was smoking a marijuana cigarette. We were quite surprised. He and a young woman were the only passengers. He wanted to know where we were going. We said Dallas. He let us know they were on their way to Fort Worth which was just on the other side of Dallas. We knew God had provided us a ride home.

As we traveled, the couple explained that they were not the Revelation Singers. They were married and had bought the bus from her parents in Nashville, Tennessee. Her folks were the Revelation Singers. The couple was taking the bus back to their home in Fort Worth. The problem was, the bus would not go over forty miles an hour so the trip from Little Rock to Dallas, which should take about five hours, actually took about twelve hours. When we got to Dallas, rather than letting us off at or near our apartment, they let us out south of Dallas on Highway20. Now it was about four a.m. and we had to walk all the way up Highway 35 to where we lived. By the time we got home, the sun was coming up and we had to get ready for work.

. . . . . .

PEOPLE THAT CARE

My church felt led to start reaching out to the poor in the city. So, the People That Care Center (PTC) was started. It was a place where food and clothing were collected and made available to those that visited the center. At that time (still 1981), I was working at a halfway house for people coming out of prison. I monitored their coming and going and somewhat guarded the premises. It was a secular organization that managed the place but I could witness to people all the time. At one point, we had a Bible study that met once a week.

I would help around the People That Care Center part-time. I didn't make much money at the halfway house, so the directors of the PTC decided to let me take one of the rooms in the building to live in. This was really necessary for someone to be there during the night because the center was in a bad part of town.

The PTC center was an amazing place for reaching out to the less-fortunate of not only Grand Prairie but even the Dallas and Fort Worth metroplex. Many people came to know Jesus through the people that served at the center.

I will be bragging on Shady Grove Church often in this book. God gathered some amazing people under the leadership of our remarkable loving pastor—Olen Griffing. It was a church on the cutting edge of innovative things God was doing.

I may not get the dates exactly right but around the late '70s, Pastor Olen really got a revelation of worship. He was reading about the Tabernacle of David in 1 Chronicles chapter 16. This became a driving force in our church.

> **1 Chronicles: 16** talks about how David took the Ark of God that had been in the Tabernacle of Moses up to Mount Zion, pitched a tent for it, and instituted 24/7 worship for thirty-three years. At Shady Grove, we believed this was the pattern of worship for the New Testament church, especially since the Apostle James in Acts 15:16-17 stated that God wanted to raise up the Tabernacle of David to reach the Gentiles. Nowadays, this style of worship is somewhat understood across many church denominations, but in the late '70s, it was only followed in remote places.

What is so special about Davidic worship? Someone said, "We don't just glance at God, but we gaze at Him." It is an abandonment of your soul unto Him. An important verse was Psalm 22:3 But

You are holy, Enthroned in the praises of Israel. We believe that when we worship, God comes in a greater measure. Pastor Olen would talk about God's manifest presence. As Christians, God is always with us, but His manifest presence is when we *experience* His presence. At Shady Grove, we would worship until His manifest presence came. This can be hard to explain sometimes but it is when something would happen in the room that could only be explained as an act of God. There may be prophecies come forth, healings, a holy awe, prolonged dancing, etc., when God was not only ministering to individuals but to the room as a whole. Even to this day I cherish this type of worship.

Chapter Eight

In 1983, three friends and I from Christ For The Nations took a trip to San Francisco. Oh, wow, I can't even remember those guys' names but I will never forget the trip. This was the first time I had been beyond the Texas border going west.

One of the guys had a friend who was a pastor in San Francisco. This pastor had contacted my friend telling him about an outreach in the streets of the city. It was called SOS San Francisco, ten days of street ministry. My friend approached me and we began to meet with two other guys to pray.

We decided we would drive out there and back rather than taking an airplane. One of the guys borrowed a large station wagon from a friend for the trip. We would take turns driving because it would take two days nonstop and those not driving could sleep. So, we took off on the trip and by the time we got to San Francisco we were worn out. I know I did not get much sleep. I can't remember exactly which route we took but the scenery was awesome. It must have been Highway 40 through Albuquerque and Flagstaff. It was in the hot summertime and I discovered heat out west is a dry heat. We stopped at the Colorado River to make sandwiches. I remember laying out the bread and before I could get the mayo on it the bread was already getting crusty and dry because of no humidity in the air. After eating, we decided to take a dip in the river. I waded about two feet into the water and could not believe how cold the water was. We got in the car and continued on into California.

We slept in a Chinese church sanctuary. We had our bedrolls with us and slept either on a bench or on the floor. An Assembly of God church hosted the outreach so every day we would meet at twelve noon and worship for about two hours. I remember the worship was really powerful. God moved among us. Then we would organize teams, generally two-by-two. We would leave the church and regroup at a predesignated park. A team went before us to set up a stage and musical equipment. The band would play music, along the line of Christian rock. There would be testimonies and a salvation message. Each day we went to a different park.

About six or seven p.m., we would then get with our partners and witness to people on the streets until about midnight. All together, we were about two hundred. I had done a lot of street witnessing in Dallas, but San Francisco was so much harder. The demonic oppression was so heavy. I don't even think I led anyone to the Lord. At the end of the ten days, about two hundred people accepted Jesus. On the last day, we had a baptism for the new believers.

One tragic thing that happened while we were there: We got word that Keith Green had died in a plane crash near his Texas home. Actually, Keith was the pilot of the plane. I think two of his children also died. Keith was a famous musician, songwriter, and head of a publication ministry. He was a real innovator of Christian music at that time. His ministry would produce albums and give them away. He would just ask for donations. This really rattled the Christian record business. Also, he would not sign autographs. His reason was that he did not feel worthy and wanted Jesus to get all the credit. Once, some friends and I went to visit his ministry and I came away with the realization that Keith was putting his fame and fortune back into the Kingdom.

We left San Francisco after the ten days to drive back to Texas. We first drove along the Pacific Coast down to San José and then turned east.

PART TWO

NEW MISSION, NEW LIFE

Chapter Nine

It was somewhere around 1982 or '83 that Pastor Olen made contact with a pastor from Communist Poland. It must have been 1982 when Pastor Olen made a trip to Katowice, Poland, to visit Pastor Carrol and his church. Olen came back with a glowing report of how God was moving in this Katowice church.

The next year, 1983, Shady Grove sent a team of seven or eight people to Poland to minister in the Katowice church. I remember meeting with the team during pre-trip prayer meetings. I was considering going but, in the end, it was just not my time. There were three of us that met with the team but did not go on the trip. I am not sure how long the team was in Poland, but the three of us would often meet to support them in prayer. The team returned with exciting reports of how God moved. Monty Smith, the associate pastor, led this team of mainly people that could teach worship, dance and the use of banners.

After the team returned, our friends Betty, Greg and I decided to continue meeting to pray for Eastern Europe. We would meet at the church three Saturdays each month. We did this for almost a year and God really burdened our hearts for Eastern Europe.

Around the beginning of 1984, I went through some deliverance sessions—I think it was about six sessions, once a week. We would pray together and God would show us things in my life that were harmful to me or holding me back from spiritual growth. We dealt with ancestral sins, sexual sins, and things that left layers of shame, rejection etc. in my life. Many heavy burdens were lifted that had hindered my spiritual growth.

One thing that really surprised me was that I got free from smoking. Here is the strange part about it. During the sessions, we never discussed or prayed about me smoking. As far as I know, these two people didn't even know I smoked. How it came about was that I just stopped desiring or needing to have a cigarette. I realized later that the smoking was not the problem but something in my life—some root during the deliverance sessions that was being medicated by nicotine—got cut off.

Meanwhile, back at Shady Grove, Pastor Olen had connected with a pastor from Yugoslavia, Pastor Joseph Sabo. The suggestion was made that Shady Grove should send a team to Pastor Sabo's church in Subotica, Yugoslavia. So, a team was assembled and we three who had been interceding were on the team. Wayne Wilks, who had been on the Poland team the year before, led the team. I can't speak enough about Wayne. He led with a remarkable sensitivity to each member's needs. His new bride, Bonnie, was on the team also. To me it was a joy watching them interact with each other since I had known them both when they were single.

We flew into Frankfurt then took a short flight to Munich. In Munich, we picked up a Volkswagen van and drove to Salzburg, Austria, to spend the night. We spent the night in a village outside Salzburg named, Großgmain (Grossmain)—the most beautiful village I have ever seen, set in the middle of steep snow-topped mountains. We were staying in a hostel/boarding house. We were told not to take pictures of the house because it was a way station for Bible smugglers. Bibles were banned in communist countries back then and there were ministries that braved the risk and brought Bibles to the underground Christians in the Eastern Soviet bloc. Although Yugoslavia was communist, Bibles were not against the law there. There were many restrictions on the churches but they somewhat had freedom within their buildings.

Let me say another grateful thing about Wayne and Bonnie Wilks. While the team was at that hostel and we were in a time of prayer,

Wayne and Bonnie washed our feet. This was their act of servitude to the team. I remember this act of humility really had an impact on me.

The next day, we drove down to Zagreb, where we spent the night in a building that was then a Bible school. The next morning, they fed us breakfast and we spent the day driving across Yugoslavia. The team had to have patience with me because I would often just start crying. I was just being overwhelmed by the fact that here I was in a country I had prayed for many times.

We spent a month in Yugoslavia on this trip. We taught and modeled worship before a few congregations—in Subotica, Senta, Zrenjanin, etc. There was a youth camp we worked in and we helped out with some physical labor around the churches.

Many profound things happened on this trip. While we were there, Pastor Sabo went to his eternal reward. This was very sad, but we did our best to comfort the family and his church. We really became connected in a profound way with the Sabo family, especially the son Viktor Sabo, who was acting pastor after his father passed.

One day we were at the church in Senta and we noticed something else profound. I think it was Wayne who noticed it. The license plate on the van we rented in Germany was SGCH-730. Now this is how we read it: Shady Grove Church, seven people for thirty days. This was just overwhelming evidence to us that we were in God's will and timing.

One day we were traveling from one city to another in the rented van. I was sitting next to Viktor. He and I got to talking about their need for foreign workers to come work with the churches. This was something I had been praying about ever since graduating from Christ For The Nations. I was so fearful that I would never be able to raise the money needed to become a missionary. So, I asked Viktor, "How much per month would it cost to live here (Yugoslavia)?"

He said. "Oh, about $200 a month."

I could not believe it. Just $200? That should not be hard for me to raise. Next, I talked to Wayne about the possibility of me coming back as a missionary. God had already been setting things up, because when Shady Grove had prayed over our team before we left, a word had come forth that one of the team members would not come back. Of course, I did have to come back to raise the $200.

Once we returned to the States, I talked to Monty Smith, the Missions pastor at Shady Grove, about being sent out. Next, the Mission's team interviewed me and decided that my opportunity would be presented before the church at the upcoming Mission's Conference. I was so excited. God was about to set me on my path of destiny.

I'm not sure exactly the date of the conference, but there was a lot of enthusiasm about my being sent to Yugoslavia, a communist country. Although there were a few missionaries that Shady Grove supported, I was the first home-grown missionary to go to the mission field.

Now Shady Grove had a unique way of raising money for missionaries. It was similar to an auction. Our name would be presented and the congregation could pledge an amount they would give monthly. The moderator would start the pledging, asking those that wanted to give to raise their hands. One by one, he would ask how much they wanted to give: $10, $25, $5, $50, $1 (children would also participate), $100, $40, etc. Someone would be adding it up. The moderator would have given a goal amount at the beginning but often hoping the final amount would exceed that goal. So, my goal was $200. Now, as I said, there was lots of enthusiasm regarding sending me out.

After the pledges were added up, over $800 a month had been pledged, plus someone said they would pay for my airline ticket. Also, there was nearly $10,000 raised to provide a Volkswagen van for the church in Subotica, Yugoslavia, where I would be working. I was to have charge of the van while I was there. This blew me away to see the giving hearts of the people of the church. Shady Grove was not a church with lots of wealthy people, but it was a *giving* church. As years passed, Shady Grove was not only known as a worshiping church, but also for the many missionaries it sent out and supported.

I decided to not leave for Yugoslavia until January 1985. I would spend Christmas with my family because it was not known when I would have a chance to come back. For me, this move was serious, and I was open to however long God wanted me to stay. I had been praying for Eastern Europe for ten years so this was so natural. I bought my plane ticket, and on January 5, 1985, my family took me to the airport to see me off. Also, there were about twenty friends from Shady Grove who came to see me off. I remember back in those days it was really a big thing when someone was leaving for the mission field and many would come to see them leave. I was so encouraged.

I remember flying to New York City into Kennedy airport but then had to catch a taxi over to LaGuardia to fly to Europe. Although I have flown through NYC since, this was the only time I had to switch airports. My stance is that if you transit without leaving the airport, then you really haven't been in the city.

· · · · · · ·

YUGOSLAVIA

On my way to Yugoslavia, I can't remember which West European airport I transited through, but I do remember entering Yugoslavia. This was the coldest winter they had had in many years. I was to fly into Belgrade but the snowstorm was so bad that our flight was diverted to Split on the Dalmatian coast. We were put in a hotel for the night and the next day flew to Belgrade. I remember even the ground in Split being frozen. The hotel was next to the Adriatic coast. The next morning, before we were to go to the airport, I walked out to look at the water and there was ice along the edge of the water. This speaks of how cold it was that winter, because there is usually never ice along the Adriatic coast even further north from the city of Split.

I flew into Belgrade and Viktor Sabo met me at the airport. We took the bus into Belgrade and caught a train to Subotica. I was freezing. I was wearing a light coat, which was perfect for Texas winter weather but was no match for how cold it was in Yugoslavia.

We got to Subotica and I was taken to the house I would be renting. They had arranged everything for me. It was a one-bedroom house behind a larger house. The rent was $30 a month. It was a nice place, real comfortable. I do remember the bathroom was hard to heat.

It might have been the next day or two days later, but Erika Radnic (Poag) came to take me into the city to look for a coat. We did not have much time because I was to meet with the young people at the church that evening. All I remember was stopping at one store and looking over their coats. When we got to the church, I noticed my money pouch was not with me. I must have left it in one of the coats I had tried on. Or at least I sure hoped that is what happened. Erika told me I would have to go the next day because the store would be closed by then. I met with the young people of the church and many spoke English. I met some guys that would become close friends in the following years I was in Yugoslavia.

The next day, Erika came to get me early so we could be at the store when it opened. Sure enough, the money was still in one of the coats I had tried on. So, I bought a really warm coat, a rough leather coat with a fur inner lining, made in Bosnia. I loved that coat.

I began to settle in and work with the church.

There was a young lady named Maria who lived at the church and took care of things. She was also head of children and youth work throughout Yugoslavia. I was to work with her and Viktor. As I said, Viktor was now the acting pastor. I helped Maria clean the church and I remember at that time there were no mops being sold in Yugoslavia. So, we would sweep the floor and get down on our knees to mop the floor with wet, soapy rags.

I also would share in the youth meetings and in order for me to preach in the church, the pastor (Viktor) would have to inform the police two weeks in advance that a foreigner was going to speak. This was so the police could have an informer there to make sure I did not speak despairingly against Yugoslavia. I would not have done that anyway because I was just blessed to be a guest in the country. The situation at that time was that I could only get ninety-day visas to stay in the country. So, I would travel out of the country but come back in a day or two.

I remember once traveling up to Budapest and I spent the night at a believer's house or in a hotel—can't remember which now—and then traveled back to Yugoslavia the next day. While in Budapest I went to a restaurant in one of the upscale hotels in the center. I ordered a generous plate of stroganoff, wine and dessert and only paid $1.25 in local currency. In those days, things were cheap in Yugoslavia and even cheaper in Hungary. Since Yugoslavs could travel to Hungary and back with no problem, they often went shopping across the border.

Yes, things were cheap in Yugoslavia but the variety was scarce. There was usually one brand of what was available: one toothpaste, one set of dishes, etc. The stores would often run out of bread and milk early in the day. There were many bakeries but you had to get in line early just to get some bread most of the time.

The year 1985 was an amazing year for me. I had some adventures I will never forget.

Once I went to the butcher shop to get some ground meat. The meat had to be ground up while I waited. I wanted two pounds. Now I had to order in kilos, but I made a calculation mistake. I thought to myself, two pounds equals four kilos. So, the butcher started grinding up the meat, wrapping it in white paper and piling them on the counter. It didn't take long for me to realize she was going over two pounds. I had mixed up my calculation; there are two pounds in a kilo not the opposite. That is why she looked at me in a strange way when I first ordered.

On one weekend, the Yugoslav Pentecostal churches were having a conference at the Bible school in Osijek. I went with my friends from Subotica. While we were there, I met a young lady from Belgrade, the capital city. She was an American and worked in the American Embassy in the capitol. She was a new Christian, having been led to the Lord by a Yugoslav Christian who also worked in the embassy. She suggested I should come down to Belgrade and visit her sometime. I especially thought this was a good idea after she told me about the commissary in the embassy where I could get all kinds of American products.

So, one morning I took the train down to Belgrade. Belgrade is about an hour-and-a-half train ride from Subotica. I got to Belgrade and walked to the American Embassy, which was about five blocks from the train station. I remember walking in front of the embassy and seeing the American flag flying in front of the building. It was like a breath of fresh air seeing that flag. I went to the employee entrance of the embassy and asked for my new friend. I remember her name was Sharron. I visited Sharron for a while and we decided to go eat. We took a taxi to a Chinese restaurant there in Belgrade. It was so nice to have Chinese food. I remember I ordered sweet-and-sour chicken and it was so good. To this day, when I go to Chinese restaurants, I usually order the same.

We went back to her apartment in the embassy and she took me to the commissary. Oh, man, was I in heaven! I got Hershey's chocolate, Miracle Whip salad dressing, and many other things. I had a box of things. Then it was time for me to leave to go back to Subotica. Sharron walked with me down to the train station. Now Sharron knew a few words in Serbian but was in no way fluent. I needed her help to get on the right train. We thought we knew which track the train was leaving from so there was a train on the track. We were there trying to discern the info on the train to determine if this was the right train or not. Then a conductor got off the train so Sharron asked him if that train went to Subotica. The man said something, and Sharron thought he said yes. Okay, so I gave Sharron a hug and got on the train.

The train left the station and started down the tracks. It passed out of Belgrade and I began to see it pass village after village. About 45 minutes down the track the ticket man came to check our tickets. He took my ticket and said something. The two or three men in the train cubicle began to laugh. They already knew I did not speak Serbian, so they were having a hearty laugh. Then one of them spoke in broken English that I was on the wrong train. This train was actually going south rather than north to Subotica. Oh, I felt so dumb.

So, I had to get off at the next stop. It was already dark, maybe seven or eight p.m. I went into the train station where I got off and to the ticket window to find out when the next train north would come through. I had already noticed this was a small station. The man said no train until about five a.m. So, I asked where the nearest hotel was. He said there was no hotel in the village. So, I realized I would need to wait in the train station for about nine or ten hours before I could catch a train. OK, so here I was. As the hours passed, I noticed the train station turned into a place where the village drunks would spend the night. They were having fun and very curious about me. Here I was with my box of goodies and not knowing what these drunks had in mind. I just asked the Lord to protect me but I was still fearful. I might have dozed off a time or two but mainly I tried to stay awake. Most of the drunks passed out or went to sleep.

Around 5:00 a.m., the train came and if I remember right, it was going on to Subotica and I did not have to switch in Belgrade. What an adventure!

In May of 1985, Pastor Olen and Syble Griffing came for a visit to Subotica. With them came Jim and Trish Morton, close friends of mine whom I had worked with at the People That Care Center. They were ministering in the churches and I would show them around. While they were there, Pastor Olen gave me two things: One was the money collected for the van that needed to be bought for the church.

The second thing was a letter and a piece of paper with instructions on it. The letter needed to be taken to a family in a city in Romania. Pastor Olen told me that it was a sensitive letter and I should make sure it was not suspicious in my luggage. I had heard stories of how risky it was to travel in communist Romania.

After they left, I made plans to go to Germany where a ministry there was going to help me buy a Volkswagen van for the church in Subotica. This was a really good time to buy a vehicle in Germany because the value of the German mark was 3 to $1.00. So I went on to Germany and the ministry helped me buy a van from a dealership in Stuttgart. I took $10,000 and bought a brand-new Volkswagen van for about 30,000 marks. I drove the van back to Yugoslavia.

I needed to smuggle that letter into Romania. I made plans to travel to Timișoara, Romania. I had the instruction sheet as to what train to take and the name of the stop where I needed to get off, the Bloc number of the apartment building, and the apartment number of the family. I was told they spoke English. So, I took a train to Belgrade and then caught the train going to Timișoara, Romania. By now I had learned to find the right trains I needed.

At that time, I had a small electric typewriter that fit in a briefcase. It was very portable. I did not know that unregistered typewriters were not allowed in Romania. So, I was very shocked at the border when the custom agents took my typewriter. They gave me a piece of paper so I could pick it up on the way out of the country. I had planned to exit the country through another border crossing but now I had to come back the way I went in. The communist regime in Romania felt that private typewriters were a threat to information control in the country.

So, I arrived in Timișoara and found a hotel near the train station. I checked into the hotel and then went to deliver the letter. The instructions I had led me right to the apartment block and the apartment was not hard to find. I knocked on the door and a man opened the door. I started speaking English to introduce myself. I found out quickly that he did not speak English. Also, he was not inviting me in. I felt it was okay to just give this man the letter, hoping that would clear up the stalemate. I pulled out the letter and gave it to him. As he opened the letter and started to read, he stepped out of the door, looked around, and then urged me to come in. His wife was there along with three children. They finished reading the letter.

We then tried to communicate the best we could. Knowing the suspicious atmosphere of Romania, I fully understood their cautiousness. After they fully read the letter, any suspicions were erased. They embraced me as being safe. At some point, the wife opened a cabinet and reached back behind some items and pulled out a Bible. I did not know it was a Bible at first because it was carefully wrapped in cloth. I guess they were clarifying to me that they were Christians. I also knew that it was illegal for them to have a Bible.

Like I said, our communication was really hard, but we did come up with a plan for another meeting. I was to come back the next day at the same time (it was evening) and someone would be there that could speak good English. So, I left and made my way back to the hotel. I had hoped to leave the next day but now I had to change plans to stay two nights in the hotel.

I woke up the next morning and I was looking out the window at the city, praying and asking the Lord what I should do until the evening meeting. While looking out the window, I noticed something strange. A car pulled into the hotel parking lot and parked. A man got out and opened the trunk lid. All of a sudden, people seemed to come from all directions and gather around the back of the car. The driver started letting people look at the items in the back of his car. They would take something and give him money. I realized I was witnessing a black-market exchange of goods.

I decided I would go outside and walk around the city. I can't remember if I ate something in the hotel restaurant or not. Once out on the streets, I began to see that things were much different than in Yugoslavia. There were very few cars on the streets. Overall, the streets were nice and broad, well-maintained, but only occasionally a car passing by. I found out later that gas was either too expensive or just not available. Also, very few families could afford a car.

I peered into the window of a butcher shop and saw that there was no fresh meat. There were some sausages hanging on a back wall but it looked like really poor quality meat. I walked into what looked like a department store. The shelves were all empty or had very few items on them. I did notice there were a lot of socks and underwear and they were all of one brand with no variety. Later, I learned that they had a sock- and underwear factory in the city. I think I remember a few dresses hanging for sale and hardly any dry goods. It really hit me as to how much the Romanian people were deprived.

As I was walking around praying for the city (because the Lord told me to prayer-walk the city), I noticed another car pull up and stop on the side of the road. A man got out and opened his trunk and once again people seemed to come out of the shadows to buy things and scurry off.

My heart was breaking. How sad that people had to live this way.

Before going to the apartment for the scheduled meeting, I went back to the hotel restaurant where I ate a large meal. So, I got to the family's apartment and was welcomed by the husband; the wife was not there. He sat me down at the kitchen table and the children were in the bedroom. The English speaker had not arrived yet. The man began to cook at the stove. I just waited, thinking he was cooking for the family. He finished cooking and set a heaping plate of food in front of me. Remember, I had just eaten an hour earlier at the restaurant. What was I to do? I could not refuse to eat. I could not communicate with him that I was not hungry. I might offend him. That was not the worst part. I looked over and the children were standing in the bedroom door, staring. They were not staring at me but at the food that sat in front of me. I could tell what was going through their minds—*We wish we could have that food.* I just knew I had been served a feast and those children never got a meal that good. My emotions ranged from honored to sorrowful for the children. I managed to slip a $5 bill under my plate.

The man handed me a gift. It was underwear and a pair of socks.

Finally, the man that spoke English arrived. He asked me to come with him to meet with a small group of Christians. We walked across the city or at least many blocks and came to another apartment. There were about eight to ten people there. We talked about many things, but I was cautious not to ask many questions. Not that I did not want to know about their lives, but there was just a spirit of suspicion over the city, and actually the whole country. Then it came time to pray. They got on their knees on the floor and the women covered their heads. I did not know what they prayed but I knew it was serious. After the meeting, the man that spoke English walked me back to my hotel. As we walked, I asked the English speaker about the peculiar gift. He told me that the man worked in the factory where the underwear and socks were made and this was an inexpensive gift he could afford.

The next morning, I caught the train back to Yugoslavia. Sure enough, at the border they gave me back my typewriter. This trip to Romania really opened my eyes to how blessed I was to have grown up in the west and how hard life was in the deep confines of communism. I was living in Yugoslavia, which was communist, and I had been to communist Hungary, but Romania was a whole different level of depravity. This had a lot to do with the evil regime of the dictator, Nicolae Ceaușescu.

In 1985, I made two more trips to Romania. That summer a team of nine people came from Shady Grove Church to minister in Yugoslavia. They not only ministered in the churches spiritually but also physically by helping with repairs.

Shortly after they arrived, Craig Carpanelli and I went on a fact-finding trip to Lugoj, Romania. We had information of a church and pastor there that had some connection to Shady Grove. If I remember right, all we had was his name and the church address. So, Craig and I took the train from Belgrade to Timişoara. Then from there we took a train to Lugoj, which is about fifty miles east of Timişoara.

Before leaving Timişoara, we went to visit that family I had taken the letter to a few months earlier. They were happy to see us but we could not speak English with them. We didn't have much time so we did not trouble them to find an English translator. I was surprised by the husband when he pulled out the $5 bill I had left under the plate the last time I was there and he gave it back to me. What was I thinking? He could have gotten in trouble trying to convert it into Lei. I look back to those trips to Romania and see how God protected this gullible American.

We had been told that the pastor in Lugoj did speak English. When we caught the train in Timişoara, there was a fourteen-year-old girl that was in our train compartment. She heard us speaking English and started to talk to us in perfect English. She said she lived in Lugoj. We talked and talked and she helped us to navigate through the streets of Lugoj until we found the church.

We may have made a mistake by befriending this young lady. Back in those days, Romanians often spied on foreigners and even their own countrymen for Communist party benefits. Either way, she translated for us. We got to the church and there was a caretaker there. They let us know that the pastor lived in another city many miles away. This was a pattern the communists followed to hinder pastors from being able to really care for their church members by having them live and work in another city. They told us that the pastor could not make a trip to Lugoj to meet with us but we could set up a future meeting.

Now our purpose of this trip was to set up a return trip in a week or so. The return trip was for two couples that were on the Shady Grove team; Wayne and Bonnie, along with Tim and Donna, to connect with this Romanian pastor to see how Shady Grove could be of help in the future. By the way, Wayne and Bonnie were leading this team like they did the 1984 team. We set a date for a week or so in the future with the expectation that the pastor would be there.

Craig and I made our way back to Yugoslavia. We actually made our way back by a different route rather than going through Belgrade. We took a northern route through Jimbolia and crossing the border near Kikinda. I still remember the old electric train or trolley-like car we rode across the border. Also, I remember in Jimbolia we went to a store to get something to drink and the only thing they had was some kind of bottled blue sugar water.

Then we made the trip to Lugoj with the Wilks and Austins to meet with that pastor. I'm not sure we accomplished much on this trip because I made another mistake. We made plans for the young girl Craig and I had connected with earlier to be our translator when we got to Lugoj. Afterwards, I saw how this was a big mistake because she was not a Christian and the pastor did not know if he could trust her or not. Yes, the pastor met with us but was really reluctant to share much with us. Now I understand it was because this girl was present.

On this third trip to Romania, the six of us were in Timișoara on Sunday and were invited to attend a church. I'm not sure how this came about but it was an eye-opening experience. First of all, we saw firsthand the amount of foot traffic on Sunday mornings in Timișoara. Remember, there were not many cars or gasoline in Romania in those days. When we got to the church, we saw and understood all the foot traffic and the overflowing trams. The church was packed out. There must have been three hundred people there.

We were told that there were packed churches all over town. We were also told that the main reason the churches were full was not so much because Romanians are so pious, but because there were very little options in Romania and they could attend church for free. Also, we understood that there was very limited teaching in the churches and the sermons had to be watered down to not upset the government mandates. These were the registered churches and not the underground churches. Remember how on my first trip to Romania I had met with that group in an apartment? That was an underground church.

So, we attended the crowded church and gave testimonies. We made our way back to Yugoslavia.

Let me further document this team's journey through Eastern Europe. The team wanted to spend a day as tourists in Budapest, Hungary; then on to Katowice, Poland; and while in Poland visit Auschwitz and Birkenau concentration camps. After Poland, I was to drive them to Berlin, Germany, where we were to visit some missionaries; and from Berlin, the team was to fly back to the States.

So, we loaded up the Volkswagen van and went and toured beautiful Budapest, Hungary. I remember the hostel where we spent the night. It was on the Danube riverfront in an old building. What was remarkable was the shower arrangement. The shower room had a sign on the door that could be turned around according to who was in the shower. The funny thing was the sign: a picture of Bob Dylan if you were male and a picture of Marilyn Monroe if you were female.

After Budapest, we drove on to Katowice, Poland, where we were to meet Pastor Carrol. He was the first pastor from Eastern Europe to visit Shady Grove Church. We ministered in their church. I cannot remember where all the team stayed, but I remember the room I was in. The room was on the second floor just above the street outside. Whenever the tram would go by, it seemed like the whole building would shake. Just hard to sleep.

Then we went to visit Auschwitz and Birkenau concentration camps. They are located in Poland not very far from each other. If you ever get the chance to visit these camps, do it. You will never be the same. It is devastating to see the cruelty men can inflict on other men. As you walk through these camps, you will notice the silence. The impact of what you are viewing will consume all your thoughts.

I don't think we were in Poland for more than three or four days. We then took off for Berlin. Now this was in the time of a divided Germany. West Germany was free but East Germany was a part of the communist bloc. We had to travel through East Germany. I remember we waited at the Poland-East German border for seven hours while they checked us out. Then on into West Berlin, crossing through the Wall.

I cannot remember how many days the team was in Europe, but it was mainly a trip to bless the churches in Yugoslavia, Romania and Poland. We would teach worship and pray for the sick. In Yugoslavia, there was physical labor needed for the churches in Subotica, Senta and Zrenjanin.

The team left for America and I drove back to Yugoslavia. On the way back, I took more of a western route through Leipzig, East Germany; then through Austria and Western Hungary. By the time I got to Vienna it was late. I realized I was not on a time-schedule, so after passing Vienna I found a place to pull over and sleep in the van. Somewhere before you get to the Hungarian border, I pulled down a tractor road, parked, and lay down on the back seat. When I woke up in the morning, I was in a corn field. I continued on, crossing the border.

As I drove through northwest Hungary, I saw a castle in the distance. I stopped to tour it. Then I traveled on to Lake Balaton, the biggest lake in Europe. I was going to swim in the lake but after seeing how dirty it was I decided not to. So, I drove on to Subotica, Yugoslavia.

PART THREE

LIFE IN YUGOSLAVIA

Chapter Ten

I would work behind the scenes with Maria Radnic and Viktor Sabo. This mostly meant cleaning the church, working with Maria in the youth camps, and going to churches with Viktor to minister. Although the van had been bought for the Subotica church, I had charge of it. One of my responsibilities was to drive around town and pick up the elderly people for church services. These were such sweet people.

Now, I was getting pulled over all the time. I was driving a bright-red van with German license plates. The police would pull me over just to check me out. I would always carry my passport with me (this was required for foreigners anyway). On my passport, my name was on two lines; the first line had Jerry Louis and then under that was Low. So, I would present the police my passport and usually they would start laughing. They would remember the Jerry Lewis movies they had viewed growing up. I learned not to fear when getting pulled over.

Viktor would often gather up some of the local pastors and we would load the van and go to conferences. One of those conferences was in Germany. After the conference was over, we drove back to Yugoslavia. In those days, crossing the Yugoslav–Austria border was a two-lane road over the mountains. It was snowing on the border and the trip up the mountain was slippery. We were even outside the van pushing as the wheels just spun. We were getting nowhere. Then a snowplow truck came up the mountain and cleared the way for us so the tires could grip the pavement.

Another time we took a trip to Zurich, Switzerland, for the World Pentecostal Conference. The conference was awesome but just being in Zurich was interesting. The drive through Italy and Switzerland was ridiculously awesome: the mountains, rivers and small villages. I do believe I saw a river flowing upstream. Must have been an optical illusion.

• • • • • •

ZUZANNA

There was a young lady in the church in Subotica that I knew of. She would often be there helping Maria. She was introduced to me as Susie but her real name was Zuzanna. She did not speak English, so we never talked. One day, Viktor's mother sent her over to the house I was renting to wash my windows. We could not really talk, so I just let her do her job.

On the outskirts of Subotica, there was a strange outdoor market. They called it the "Black Market" because there were allowances made for selling items that had come across the border illegally. Anything from clothing to food items and many other things. There would be items from Hungary, Poland, Russia, etc. Many Poles would travel throughout the Soviet Bloc countries in their little trailer houses and sell all kinds of things. Zuzanna's family had a booth set up there where they sold sweaters. I would go there often and Zuzanna would walk around with me and help me negotiate when buying items, but we still really couldn't talk to each other or have a conversation.

Shortly after that, I heard she went to England to be a domestic worker for a family with children. A few months later, I learned the full story when she came back speaking acceptable English. What happened was that in order to learn English, she went to England and immersed herself in the culture. This was the quickest way to learn English. After one-and-a-half months, she learned enough conversational English that when she came back we could talk to each other. Her father had passed away and so she had come back to attend the funeral and be with her family.

I was just now learning the Hungarian or Serbian languages, the two prominent languages in that region, but I was really discovering that I am just not a language learner.

Meanwhile, every time there was an event at the church or just regular church services, I would go out in the Volkswagen van and pick up the elderly. They did not speak English but it was fun using whatever few Hungarian words I could pronounce. They would often share cakes and pastries with me they had made. One day, when I was about to load up the elderly to take them back home, Maria asked me (actually, she *told* me. Maria never *asked* you to do anything!) to take Zuzanna to her home also. Usually, Zuzanna road her bicycle across town to the church but that day she was on foot. One of the elderly women lived near her home, so it just made sense. As I would stop to let someone out, Zuzanna would help them get out of the van. She now knew enough English that we even chitchatted some. Zuzanna was the last one to be let off, so I told her, "I could pick you up each time and you will not have to ride your bicycle across town." She agreed.

Since Zuzanna was always at the church doing odd jobs for Maria, I thought maybe she could help me with picking up the elderly. I talked to Maria about this and she also agreed. So, it happened. Zuzanna started helping me with the elderly. I would go pick her up first and then she would help them in and out of the van.

Zuzanna and I began to talk more and more. There were many young people in the church and about half of them could speak English. Zuzanna was just really enthusiastic about learning English so she would always be asking me to correct her English. Often, she would sit next to me in church and translate what was being said.

One evening, after dropping off the elderly, I asked Zuzanna if she would like to go back into town to a place that sold French fries. She said yes so we went and got French fries. We call that our first date.

It did not take long before we got serious. I think Zuzanna was more serious at first than I was. I was mainly just enjoying her friendship. Then she informed me she needed to go back to England to finish the time she had committed to work with the family there. I knew I would miss her and had thoughts of, *well, we will just go on with our normal lives.* She was to go back there for about three months. We planned to write letters back and forth.

As the weeks began to go by after she left, I was surprised how much I was missing her. I noticed my letters to her began to get really "flowery." I am not an expressive person, but I was amazing myself at what I was writing. I sure wish she and I had saved those letters. I really think I fell in love with her through the letters.

Now I must bring out something here that is important. My friend, Pastor Viktor Sabo, cautioned me that he did not feel this relationship was good because Zuzanna had not been a Christian very long. I highly respected his advice, so I talked to the Lord about it. The Lord clearly said, "I am going to make a woman-of-God out of her." Looking across the years, that has been such reassurance to me. I have seen God do it far above what I could have imagined.

While Zuzanna was in England, there were two ministry trips organized by Maria Radnic. We first did a trip through the Slavonija area of Croatia, Yugoslavia, preaching and teaching in the village churches. There was an American named John McGeorge who was teaching at the Bible Institute in Osijek, Yugoslavia. Maria, God's gifted organizer, led the group and there were two or three musicians that led worship. I would give my testimony and John would preach. We would stay in church buildings or in someone's home overnight. Some of these churches were in a member's home. They fed us and we enjoyed fellowship with the church members. I cannot remember the full result of the trip, but they were encouraged, and we were too. The second trip was organized for us to visit the churches of southern Hungary. Some of the churches in Hungary were larger, but it was the same pattern of ministry.

· · · · · ·

WEST BERLIN

I think it was in the spring of 1986 that I went to a wedding in West Berlin, Germany. It was Nelly Sabo's wedding and Viktor's family was going. Nelly and Alex had decided to be married in Berlin at a special church there. We were to travel on the train from Subotica through Budapest, Hungary; Bratislava, Czechoslovakia; and then through East Germany. But there was a problem with me traveling this route as an American. I was told that I would have no problems at the Hungarian and Czech borders, but I would need a special visa to travel through East Germany. We were to leave on the train on Friday morning. I was told I had to get the visa from the East German embassy, because it could not be given to me at the border. At that time, I had use of the Volkswagen van, so I went down to Belgrade to the East German embassy on Wednesday. I got there and saw a notice on the front door that the embassy was only open on Tuesdays and Thursdays. Oh, wow, I wasted a trip. I realized I still had another day but I didn't want to spend the night in Belgrade. I went back to Subotica and along with Viktor's advice I decided to drive up to Budapest and go to the East German embassy there and get the visa. I would then park the van at a friend's house, get a hotel room, and catch the train as it came through Budapest, therefore meeting up with the Sabo family. So, I got to the EG embassy in Budapest and there was a sign saying they are closed on Tuesdays and Thursdays. I slapped my forehead and thought of how insane this was.

You have to realize how hard it was back then to make phone calls outside of the country. I would have had to try and get the right phone numbers to the embassies and then stand in line at the post office to get a line out of the country to make a call. Actually, that might have been less trouble in the end.

After seeing that I was not going to get a visa, I had to decide what to do. I could go back to Subotica and just forget about going to the wedding or I could risk being turned around at the East German border. I decided on the second option. I got a hotel room there near the train station. Weird hotel room. The room was small and although it had a shower in the room, the toilet was down the hall of the hotel. The shower was private, but the toilet was public. Now I needed to go meet a pastor friend of Viktor's so we could park the van at someone's house so it would be safe for four days. As I was coming down the stairs at the hotel, I slipped and fell, twisting my ankle. It was hurting, but I needed to meet the pastor. I hobbled on down the stairs and met the man in the lobby. We drove across town to the family's house where I was to park the van. Once we parked it, the pastor informed me we needed to walk many miles to catch the tram to get back to the hotel. My ankle was beginning to really hurt. It was late and I could tell the pastor was irritated at me because I was slowly hobbling along. It was late when we got to the hotel. I made it upstairs to my room and tried to go to sleep. My ankle was hurting and was swollen. So, I turned on the cold water in the shower, lay down on the floor, and stuck my leg under the cold water. This helped soothe the pain and swelling. I was able to get a little sleep.

The following morning, I checked out and went to catch the train. Sure enough, I met up with the Sabo family and we began the long train ride toward Berlin. So, the time of reckoning came as we approached the East German border. Would I be denied entry into East Germany? The border agent took my passport and stamped it for me to enter as if it was just routine. We were all relieved that I could continue on and did not have to take a train back home.

We got to West Berlin and I was taken to where I was to stay. There was a missionary who lived in Berlin that I had met when he came and taught in a youth camp in Yugoslavia the year before. I would be staying with him. His name was Sam Cook and he was an African-American, I think from North Carolina. He had a ministry to the immigrants in Berlin. At that time, the Soviets were sending immigrants into West Berlin, trying to cause problems for the west part of the city. The Soviets did not let their citizens go to the West but rather people could pass through East Berlin to West Berlin from Third World countries. So, those that could not legally enter the western countries, through loopholes they could enter through Berlin.

Anyway, Sam had a ministry to these immigrants. One evening, while staying with him, I went to a weekly meeting he had arranged to minister to them. Sam asked me to give my testimony. I can't remember what I had to say but at the end eleven Nigerian men came forward to give their lives to Jesus. God, You are so amazing! Now I knew why I was having so much trouble getting to Berlin. The wedding took place and all was good.

• • • • • •

ZUZANNA IS BACK

Zuzanna finished her time in England and I went to the airport in Belgrade to pick her up. As I waited outside customs as she processed through, we were so excited looking through the glass at each other we just could not wait to embrace. She came out and of course we were so happy. But there was a problem. Big problem: She discovered that she did not have her passport. I can't remember at what point on the way back to Subotica we discovered this, but we went back to the airport. They could not find it. It had not been turned in and I think the personnel shift had changed.

Zuzanna had to go to the police station in Subotica to start the process of replacing it. We came to find out that a Yugoslav passport was highly valued on the black market. At that time, with a Yugoslav passport you could just about get into any country. The police agent, of course, was suspecting she had sold it on the black market. They were not going to issue her another passport. Instead, she was called in for an interrogation. This was a very scary ordeal for her and it left a mark on her, for sure. One of Zuzanna's brothers, Jozef, found out about this and it turned out he knew the police chief. The next day, Zuzanna was told to go in to get her new passport processed.

I am so thankful for her brother and his intervening for her, but it was another lesson for me on how things are done in communist countries: Who do you know that can circumvent rules and regulations?

I asked Zuzanna to marry me and she said yes, so we started making plans for the wedding. At that time in Yugoslavia, church weddings were not honored by the government. All weddings had to take place in the city hall or court. There was a marriage official that had to officiate the ceremony. Usually, what Christians would do is to also have a church wedding. So, basically, we started planning two wedding ceremonies. Upon applying with the city of Subotica for the state wedding, we ran into a problem. They informed us that we needed permission from the national level State Department in Belgrade for a Yugoslav citizen to marry a foreigner. So, we made the trip to Belgrade to meet with the State Department. They gave us the needed paperwork and we returned to Subotica. We returned to the City Hall to present the authorized paperwork and they would not accept it as being correct. They basically said that the State Department's authorization did not meet their criteria needed to allow the wedding. The two agencies had two different policies.

So here we were, having already set a date, and now we had to cancel it. Then Zuzanna's older brother, Istvan, suggested we talk to his lawyer. So, we went to see the lawyer and explained the situation. I do not know what the lawyer did, but when we returned to his office a few days and $250 later (back then, and in Yugoslavia, that was a lot of money) the situation had been cleared up and we had the city's okay to get married.

Let me backtrack just a bit here and tell an interesting story. When we decided to get married, in those days most homes, of course, did not have telephones, and definitely no internet. In order to inform my parents, I had to go to the main post office in town, because they were the only ones with an international phone line. I had to wait in line for an available booth. Now, you had to first give the clerk the desired number you were trying to reach and they dialed it for you and then yelled out the booth number. You had to hurry to the right booth and pick up the receiver before the party you were trying to reach did, because you did not want to take a chance of them hanging up thinking it was a prank or wrong number. My mother answered and I shared the big news with her. The first thing she asked, and really the only thing: "She is not a communist, is she?" I assured her that Zuzanna was no communist and then she was happy.

So, we set the wedding for July 19, 1986.

The city required that if you were also having a church wedding that the city wedding had to come first. So, on July 19th, in the morning, we were married in the City Hall, which is a really beautiful place. Then we went to a restaurant with Zuzanna's family and had a wedding meal together. Five hours later, we met at the church for the church wedding.

The people of the church went out of their way to make this a big occasion. In the Yugoslav (Balkan) culture, Christian weddings are not just a family thing but a church event also. Viktor Sabo was my Best Man, and Mack Kingsbury, a visiting evangelist from England, conducted the ceremony. Kingsbury had been the person who had helped Zuzanna get work and study the language in England. Zuzanna's brother, Istvan, gave her away since her father had passed away.

Our honeymoon consisted of spending two nights in a hotel in a city not far from Subotica and then we drove to a remote village in Hungary where we helped in a youth camp. I remember that village was so cute and have always wanted to return there. All I remember was that it had a long name starting with a P, and I have not been able to find it on any maps. There was a non-Christian family in the village that had an extra room where we stayed. Their home did not have indoor plumbing and the toilet was an outhouse in the back yard. To get to the toilet, you had to pass by their dogs (chained up) that would bark their heads off at you. It was a crazy situation.

Let me interject something here on how God led me in my path to marriage. Before I became a Christian, I had some relationships based on lust. These actions I have repented and asked God to sever the connections that were linked there. After getting out of prison in 1977, I pledged to not fall into lust again. While in Bible school in 1978, I dated a godly lady for maybe ten months. As previously mentioned, our callings took us in different paths. I went on for the next five years just being awkward around ladies, which I believe in the end was a protection. I look back and see now how I was being protected by the Lord for the lady He had for me.

In the last year before moving to Yugoslavia, I dated a lady that my sister had introduced me to. (You know how relatives worry about your singleness.) We dated off and on for several months. In our relationship, I had to set the boundaries. Looking back, I see this was a big test and I am so glad the Lord helped me to stay clean.

I can't remember when it was, but I heard a speaker once tell of his experiences of finding a mate. He spoke of how he had come to such a point of dating or not dating frustration that he told the Lord, "I am just going to go 100 percent after You in the freedom of my singleness and if You want me to marry, You will just have to bring her to me."

So that is what he did and really started enjoying the fruits of ministry. Before long, he noticed a lady involved in the same ministry he was doing, and they really worked together well. He described how as he was seeking and putting the Kingdom first, he looked over and noticed this lady walking beside him with the same desires and love for the Lord. One day, he just reached over and took her hand. When I heard that story, I told the Lord, that is what I want. As Zuzanna began to help me with the elderly of the church, one day I wondered if that speaker's story was actually playing itself out before me (or beside me). As they say, "The rest is history."

Chapter Eleven

Now married, Zuzanna and I really begin to do ministry together.

In the fall of 1986, Charles Duke, an astronaut from Apollo 16, came to do a tour of Yugoslavia. He wanted to encourage Christians in the churches by giving his testimony and showing a film of him landing and walking on the moon. Zuzanna and I were asked to provide transportation for him, his wife and another man traveling with him. This was exciting for us to get to know them. The churches were full everywhere he spoke.

While in Belgrade, he wanted to go visit Marshal Tito's grave. (Tito had been a World War II war hero who helped fight the Nazis in Yugoslavia and became dictator after the war.) So, I drove him and a few others to the grave, which is housed in a special building in Belgrade. This was special for me to be able to visit Tito's grave and memorial because I had studied his life and knew his influence on the Balkans.

Years later, while driving around in Dallas, I noticed an announcement in front of a church that Charles Duke would be speaking there. So, Zuzanna and I went to the meeting. Although it had been over twenty years, he remembered us and the experiences we shared in the former Yugoslavia.

Before Zuzanna and I got married, there was also another time we provided transportation for a famous person. The friend I had mentioned above, Sharron Cook, who had worked at the American Embassy in Belgrade, had contacted Scott Wesley Brown. Brown was a Christian musician, songwriter and recording artist in Nashville. She suggested to him that he should come perform in the Yugoslav churches. So, he said yes. We talked to Maria about organizing the tour. For some reason, she couldn't do it but her sister Valerie set him up to play in three or four churches, He came along with two other friends. One guy was a producer in Nashville and the other was a Christian radio disc jockey from Florida. The amazing thing for me was listening to them talk. I was familiar with the popular Christian musicians in the States. These guys talked about these Christian artists in the first person, as friends. They were saying things like so-and-so is planning a new album; so-and-so is on tour in California and needs a bass player; or they talked about how two or three artists could put together a tour in the near future. It was so interesting to hear how these concerts are arranged.

In the late fall of 1986, Zuzanna and I went to the U.S. for six months. My family got to meet Zuzanna. Our church, Shady Grove, went to great lengths to host us. Shady Grove really knew how to take care of their missionaries. Zuzanna and I helped around the church and she even took some classes in the Bible school they had at that time. I remember her coming out of class one day laughing. I asked what she was laughing about. It seems that during the class the teacher had used the expression, "Bless their socks off," and she burst out laughing at the thought of their socks falling off. Then everyone started laughing at her when they realized how she understood the expression as a foreigner.

During this time in America, we had become pregnant. Our six months was up, so we returned to Yugoslavia in the spring of 1987. The mission's department had given me a strong directive to take a year and learn the Serbian language. We could do ministry, but I was given a year to learn the language. Upon returning to Yugoslavia, we found the nearest language school for foreigners was in Novi Sad, about forty-five minutes away from Subotica.

• • • • • •

TEMERIN

There was a couple who had a rental house in Temerin, a small town near Novi Sad. They had started a church there but had moved down to Macedonia to pioneer a new church. By moving there, we no longer had the use of the Volkswagen van in Subotica. (That van had been bought for the church in Subotica) We no longer had a vehicle, and I would have to take the bus into Novi Sad to go to school. So, we summed this up and decided to move to Temerin. The small church would actually meet in the home we were renting and sometimes in the home of one of the other members. They asked us to become the assistant pastors.

I must tell about the bus ride from our home to Novi Sad and back. I think I was attending classes three or four days a week. The ride into Novi Sad was usually smooth, taking about twenty-five minutes. The ride home was very eventful because it was around the time people got off work. At the bus station, everyone would be bunched together at the dock because when the bus to Temerin came, there was a rush to scramble in to get a seat. There would be so many people taking this bus that I was lucky if I ever got a seat. Then once everyone got on, it was so tight that you were pressed as tight as sardines. Sometimes I would do some prayer-walking in Novi Sad just so I could take a later bus that was less crowded. Zuzanna never knew when I would be getting home. We did not have cell phones in 1987 and '88, or even a home phone.

I remember one time the bus was so tight and I was near the back where it would bounce a foot or more when hitting big potholes. We would go up and the floor of the bus would go down before we did. So, it hit a big bump and we all went up but we were so packed and jammed together that my feet stayed off the floor, because the people squeezed against me were holding me up. I slowly slid down.

Along about this time, something odd but amazing happened. There was a young African student I met in Subotica shortly after first moving there. His name was Taiwo and he would often come to the youth meetings. For some reason, Taiwo and I had met up in Novi Sad. We decided to go by and visit the Pentecostal church there. The church in Novi Sad was one of the few larger churches in Yugoslavia (about 120 members). It was not during a service time, but we just wanted to drop in. We went into the office and there was the secretary and another man. The secretary introduced the man who was a young German. She said he was asking questions about God and salvation. She asked if we could answer some of his questions. Now here was the situation: he only spoke German, the secretary spoke Serbian and German, Taiwo spoke Serbian and English but not German, and I only spoke English. In the end, we led this young man to accept Jesus by using all three languages. I spoke to Taiwo in English, Taiwo interpreted into Serbian, the secretary interpreted into German—and he was born again.

The language class was strange. I think it was a four–month class. My classmates were mainly foreign students who had come to study in Yugoslavia. Most spoke English. During the four months, there were eight different teachers. I never knew why they kept changing teachers. Each had their own method of teaching. It was confusing. Even though I was in this class, I was still having trouble learning the language. After the four months, we were given a one-on-one oral exam in order to pass the class. I did my best, but I know I was really sloppy with my answers. They must have passed me just because I had paid the money for the class.

It was time for our first-born to arrive. Asa was born on December 3, 1987. (As a matter of fact, today—the very day I am writing this—is December 3, 2020. Happy Birthday Asa, you are so special.) At this time, I had been meditating on King Asa in 2 Chronicles 14-16. I was amazed at how King Asa had led Judah back to the Lord. These verses really stood out to me:

2 Chr. 15:12 They entered into the covenant to seek the Lord God of their fathers with all their heart and soul; [13] and whoever would not seek the Lord God of Israel was to be put to death, whether small or great, man or woman. [14] Moreover, they made an oath to the Lord with a loud voice, with shouting, trumpets, and with horns. [15] All Judah rejoiced concerning the oath, for they had sworn with all their heart and had sought Him earnestly, and He let them find Him. So the Lord gave them rest on every side.

So, before Asa was born, I told Zuzanna that I wanted to name our baby Asa if it was a boy. She agreed. Now here is the odd part: I have distant cousins named Asa: Asa Low Sr., Jr., and III. At first, I thought this might be weird, but as I thought about it more, I realized many times names are continued down through the generations of families. Here is an interesting note: Asa Low Jr. has a school in Mansfield, Texas, named after him.

I must tell something about the Temerin pastor and his family. It was Christmas 1987 and we were having church in our home. (In the Balkans, Christmas is more of a church event than a family event.) So, we were waiting for the pastor and his family to arrive. Now you have to realize neither us nor the pastor had a phone. So, they did not come, and we did not know why. The next day we found out why. The pastor's wife was pregnant, and the baby decided it wanted to be born on Christmas Day.

Now here is the interesting thing about this baby boy being born then. In former Yugoslavia, there are two Christmases: the Catholic/Protestant Christmas on December 25 and then on January 6 the Orthodox Christmas. This family already had a daughter who had been born on Orthodox Christmas Day a few years earlier. Now they had two children, each born on one of the two Christmas Days.

That is not the end of this story. The family's last name actually means Christmas in the Serbian language. To me this was so fascinating. We lost contact with this family, but I often wonder what has happened with them. Of course, we had no experience co-leading a church, but also we were newlyweds, with a new baby. Long story short—that arrangement was not longlived.

· · · · · ·

GOD'S WAYS ARE NOT OUR WAYS

It just so happened that at this time Pastor Olen and wife Syble were visiting us. They were the senior pastors of Shady Grove Church and where there for a pastoral visit. They helped us lay out the plan for this change. Such a move was costly. Yugoslavia went through a 600 percent inflation period that year. The $600 a month support from Shady Grove was no longer enough to live on. This was part of a larger problem. Yugoslavia was in ethnic and economic turmoil and had become increasingly destabilized. Pastor laid out a plan for us. We would go back to the States for a season with the objective of raising more support to come back in about a year fully funded. Zuzanna and I agreed this was a good plan. Little did we know that we would get trapped in America.

The Shady Grove Missions Department facilitated our reentry into the United States. This was a tremendous blessing, especially since we had a ten-month-old and Zuzanna was three months pregnant at that time.

I was heartbroken. I did not want to leave. No doubt, the Serbian area of former Yugoslavia had taken a piece of my heart. Even to this day, I find myself often praying for Serbia.

PART FOUR

TRAPPED IN AMERICA

Chapter Twelve

I can't remember the exact date, but it was in the month of October 1988 that we moved to the States and into a small one-bedroom apartment near the center of Grand Prairie, Texas. Asa was ten months old and Zuzanna was pregnant. I found a job as a courier of documents and packages. It didn't take long for me to realize that because of my lack of education and experience, I had to settle for low-paying jobs. I had an associate degree in Practical Theology from Christ For The Nations, but I just did not see myself working in a church in whatever position I might fit. I just had too many hurts from having had to leave the mission field.

Then came 1989 and Gordon was born on February 19. I remember how we came up with Gordon's name. One day we were on our way to Christ For The Nations to attend a session. Zuzanna and I knew we wanted this new child to be named after my father; that is, his middle name would be Olas, but we hadn't come up with a first name yet. As we were in the car on our way, we were talking about Gordon Lindsey, the founder of Christ For The Nations. All of a sudden, Zuzanna and I both looked at each other and said, "Gordon! That is a name that would go with Olas." So, we believe Gordon Olas Low was a name divinely given in that instant.

Gordon is fourteen months younger than Asa. Because they are so close in age, they grew up together sharing most of the same experiences. Gordon and Asa are so different in character, but they grew to be real buddies. They had their times when they fought but overall they played together well. They really entertained each other.

With Gordon now being born, we needed a larger place to live. We moved to the Misty Hollow apartments not too far from Six Flags amusement park in Arlington. It had two bedrooms so the boys could have their own room. Shortly after moving there, Zuzanna's brother Jozef came to stay with us. He was going to flight training school in Fort Worth. He was hoping to go back to Yugoslavia and get a pilot job. While he was in school, the war broke out in Yugoslavia so he ended up settling in America.

· · · · · ·

THE UNRAVELING OF THE SOVIET BLOC AND OUR LIFE IN AMERICA

In 1989 and 1990, the Soviet Bloc of nations began to fall. First Poland, and then Romania. I remembered having prayer-walked Timişoara, Romania, where the people first rose up to overthrow the communist government. Back during the time I was in Yugoslavia, I met a man from Texas who was traveling back and forth into Romania. Sometime in 1990, I decided to go meet with him because he lived in Duncanville, just south of Dallas. I can't remember his name but I will never forget what he had to tell me. He had connected with some underground Christians in Timişoara and had taught them about prayer-walking. He inspired them to go to the government building and pray around them. This was between the time I had been there in 1985 and the revolution of December 1989. This was another confirmation to me of how God always sends the intercessors first before the victory.

By now it was 1990. Zuzanna and I were asked to serve on the Mission's Prayer Team at Shady Grove. We would meet once a week and pray for the missionaries sent out from or associated with the church. We had many missionaries out in the field by now. We had sent a number of people to China as English teachers. Some went to the jungles of Guatemala. Others to Czechoslovakia, and I think the Wilks by now had moved to the Ukraine.

We covered the missionaries with prayer. Often, we prayed for things regarding their situation they could not share openly. Many times, in prayer, the Lord would give us prophesies, scriptures and directions to pass on to them. Even more, I saw the power of intercession to fuel the strength of missions and hold up the arms of the missionaries.

When Asa and Gordon were about three and two we moved again. We moved to East Dallas off of Military Parkway. I took a job with a Baptist church as a janitor. The job came with a house provided that was right behind the church building. It didn't pay much but we had no rent to pay. The church building itself was large, but the congregation was small—maybe forty to fifty on Sunday mornings. The auditorium would seat at least two hundred. It was a traditional church and they were feeling the effects of people exiting the traditional type of worship. They had recently hired a new pastor, and he and I became friends, although we had theological differences.

It was great to just walk across the alley to go to work each day. Often Asa and Gordon would be in the building with me as I would be cleaning. The boys had so much fun exploring the many unused rooms throughout the connected buildings. The church members were hoping we would join the church, but we continued to drive to Shady Grove every Sunday and for special events.

I have to tell about an incident that happened while working at the Baptist church. There was one day when Asa and I were walking to another part of the building and Gordon was off in a back room playing. I jokingly said to Asa, "Come, Asa, let's sneak off and leave Gordon behind." Asa started crying and said, "I don't want to leave my brother behind."

I was heartbroken as I realized how insensitive I was. Asa taught me a lesson I will never forget. I realized this joke was in such bad taste that I was ashamed of myself. Remember, Gordon and Asa were two and three at that time.

We were still having a hard time meeting our financial obligations so Zuzanna got an occasional job as a court translator for Serbians that had to go to court in Dallas. Also, she worked for Berlitz Language School. She had an assignment to teach a businesswoman Hungarian. Then there was an opening for Zuzanna to go to Hungary for about two months to translate for a ministry that conducted a music school for East European students. These odd jobs for Zuzanna helped.

Also, at this time (1990-'91) I started learning more and more about computers. I had a few friends who built computers, so I began to learn from them in order to build myself a personal computer. Sometimes I would help other people with their computers. Once I went to a used computer auction and bought some random parts and was able to not only upgrade my personal computer but build one or two other computers.

I developed a side hustle of buying parts and assembling functional computers. I would then put an advertisement in a local paper letting people know I had computers for sale. I did not make much money, but I was sure learning a lot about computers.

During this time, Gordon had a big-wheel tricycle that was low to the ground. You know, one of those made from plastic. He was riding it in the alley between the church building and our house. One of the church members drove into the alley and, not seeing Gordon, ran over him with his pickup. I think one of the wheels ran over Gordon's leg because his leg was broken, he had a gash on his head, and some bruises here and there. We were just so thankful he was alive. He could have been killed. The man rushed Gordon and Zuzanna to the hospital emergency room where Gordon received several stitches on his head and had his leg reset and a cast put on. He had some crutches to help him walk. He must have been three years old.

The workload as a janitor for the church was beginning to be less and less. People just kept leaving the church. I found a part-time job as a delivery driver. I met with the church committee and worked out a deal where they would pay me less but I would also commit to working less. The workload was just getting so small that I could accomplish everything in one day. It was Christmas season so Zuzanna got a part-time job working retail at Foley's department store.

Zuzanna had a part-time job, I had two part-time jobs, and we were juggling caring for the boys. There was a Methodist church nearby that had a daycare center for children so Asa and Gordon would stay there when we both had to work. Every Sunday, we would drive across Dallas to go to church at Shady Grove. Also, once a week we would drive to the church for the mission's prayer meeting.

Now in Yugoslavia, the country was at war. The Croats and Slovenes had declared independence and the Serbs were using the Yugoslav army apparatus to try and hold the country together. The Serbs were mainly trying to protect those Serbian people living in Croatia and Bosnia. Because of the location of Slovenia, it was hard for the Serbs to send in a ground army. Either way, the war was getting really intense.

Here is where I really felt trapped in America. This war was ripping my heart out. I would tell the elders at church to send us back so we could help with the refugees or just help in any way we could. They just did not feel peace about sending us back. And to get to the truth of the matter, I was going through a dark spiritual battle because my passion and the realities of life were not matching up. "Why, God, why?" I had spent many years praying for Eastern Europe, God sent me to the Balkans, and I got to walk the land and pray. Now the Balkans was falling apart and I was trapped in America. We had to stop meeting with the Shady Grove Missions team because I was a mess.

After the 1992 Christmas season, Zuzanna took a full-time job with Foley's. She started receiving promotions and was asked to move from the Preston store to the Irving Mall store. We must have stayed another year in East Dallas living behind the church where I was a janitor. In the summer of 1993, Zuzanna became pregnant again. We were making more money now, so we decided to give up the janitor job and move closer to Zuzanna's job. We found a place less than a mile from Irving Mall. The rent was reasonable and our friend Joyce, a member from Shady Grove Church, lived next door. It was great to live next to her. She had given us a car when we first moved back from Yugoslavia and had a heart of gold. Every time I mowed my yard, I would mow hers also. Asa and Gordon were six and five years old now.

Joy was born March 31, 1994. Joy was already named even before Asa was born. We had decided that if we had a girl, we would name her Joy. There was a woman of God named Joy who had influenced Zuzanna and me spiritually and we just felt like honoring her by naming a girl after her. Back during the '70s, '80s and '90s, she brought deep teaching to the Body of Christ. Maybe our Joy's name was prophetic because she brought great joy to our family. As a little girl, she was so cute with her curly blond hair. Her middle name Evangeline just really fit between Joy and Low. My favorite poem is "Evangeline" by Henry Wadsworth Longfellow, published in 1847.

The house on Harvard Street was great for us. There was a big tree in the front yard and Asa and Gordon climbed all over it. I was still doing delivery jobs and Zuzanna just kept getting promoted at Foley's. Also, I was building and selling used computers.

• • • • • •

THE TIME IS NOT YET...

Somewhere about this time, maybe 1995, I would meet with a group before church. We were individuals interested in taking the Gospel into the marketplace. One Sunday morning, Paul, the leader of the group, asked us to describe what we felt was our destiny or vision for the future. As I was waiting my turn and trying to think of what I would say, I heard the Lord speak in my mind. First, I knew it had to include my burden for the Balkans. I heard the Lord say, "Seek my plans not your own," then I listened as my mouth said to the group, "I want to be trusted by the Lord to know and work His plans for the Balkans."

To everyone in the room I could tell that it didn't really register; but I was stunned. That is a noble statement, but then the Lord said to me, "Son, you are not ready." I knew deep inside He was right and that it may take years to get ready. Also, there was a peace in my heart, that yes, we would go back to the Balkans someday.

At this time, I also felt that the Lord wanted me to become more disciplined in praying for the Balkans, but it was some years later, in 2008, that I began a systematic plan. Each week I researched one of the twelve countries of the Balkans and put together a weekly Prayer Blog. These countries were: Albania, Bosnia and Herzegovina, Bulgaria, Croatia, Greece, Kosovo, Macedonia, Montenegro, Romania, Serbia, Slovenia, and the European part of Turkey. I would contact pastors in the countries asking them for prayer needs in their city or country. As the years passed, I built up a list of over one hundred intercessors around the world who actively prayed with me through the blog. I maintained a weekly blog praying for the Twelve Balkan nations until 2018, when a new season began in our lives.

The war in the Balkans had come to an uneasy end. Although the Serbian areas held onto the name Yugoslavia, there were now new countries of Slovenia, Croatia, Bosnia and Macedonia. At this time, 1995, Montenegro and Kosovo remained part of Serbia. There were many times when I would be deeply moved in prayer for these countries. The burden for the Balkans remained upon me. Many times, during my twenty-five years in America, I would be in a glorious worship setting where the Holy Spirit was all around and I would start to pray, intercede or just ask the Lord to let such deep worship happen in the Balkans. I would also ask the Lord to send us back to show them.

This is when I would really feel trapped in America. Most of the time, the Lord was silent, or He would just say the time is not yet. And I would wonder when.

In 1996, Shady Grove opened a prayer room or house of prayer. Houses of prayer are common nowadays but as far as I know this was a first in Dallas. They named it All Nations House of Prayer or ANHOP. It was modeled after the International House of Prayer in Kansas City (IHOP). If you are not familiar with houses of prayer, they are places set aside for 24/7 day and night prayer or as many hours as they have staff.

Now I have always loved attending prayer meetings. I have seen God move through people meeting in prayer for years. Whenever God sees the united prayers of His people, He listens and acts on their behalf. God responds to the petitions of His people.

In many ways, a house of prayer is different than a regular prayer meeting. Usually there are musicians playing and singing to the Lord. Notice I said *to the Lord*; they are not in performance mode for people. The people that are in the audience or in the room are usually in private meditation and prayer on their own. More like worship rather than a time of petition, although it can lead to individual or corporate petitions or intercessions made unto the Lord. There often are times when the room comes into unity and prayers are made for a common theme, like prayer for the city, country, the sick, etc.

For many years, Shady Grove had been championing worship modeled after what King David had set up during his reign. The house of prayer actually took that concept to the fullest level of 24/7 or, as I indicated above, match the hours that their capacity allowed. Shady Grove was for a few years able to do the 24 hours all 7 days a week.

One day at church, some of the elders were praying over us and one of them had a word that God was going to give me a job that would bring great self-respect. Although I enjoyed the delivery jobs, they were not considered jobs of dignity. I was also wearing out my car because I had to use my own vehicle. There was an advertisement in the newspaper for a computer teacher. I thought to myself, *I have built computers, bought and sold them and even helped a few people learn how to use the software. Surely, I could share my knowledge with others.*

I applied for the job and was surprised when they hired me with no teaching experience. The job consisted of teaching adults how to use a computer. The business was a housing management company that mainly managed low-rent, low-income apartment complexes. They had charge over a large complex in far West Dallas near Singleton and Loop 12. They had applied for a grant to help with the education of the residents. With computer skills being very important in new emerging jobs, they wanted to develop a school for that purpose. They also had a class for helping people get their GED so they could finish high school. This was really geared toward helping people get re-employed. So, I would be teaching adults. It turned out to be mainly unwed mothers that were predominately African-American and Hispanic. Although most were of low-income, often there would be one or two professionals in each class. Generally, each class would have twenty students.

After I realized I had the job, I also realized I really did not know how to teach. That is, I didn't know the dynamics of teaching. I remember really getting serious with the Lord and asking for His help. "Lord, I need Your wisdom."

This is where the house of prayer became an important part of my life. I knew I needed God to help me overcome many inadequate things in my life: shyness, introversion, speaking in front of people, awkward speech, and bad grammar. I was learning to just come before the Lord and rest in Him. Letting the Lord embrace my heart and the Holy Spirit speak to my mind. Then I knew very little about resting in the Lord like I do now. I truly see now how that in that place of rest He prepares us for the task of our life assignments. So once or twice a week I would go spend about two hours in the prayer room.

Once I started teaching, I noticed the Lord really helping me. It was amazing to watch Him teach computer skills through me to these students. I knew it was Him not me. (I just have to stop here and thank the Lord for helping me through that time.)

I would start each new class by giving my testimony. At the end, I would conclude it by saying something like this: "I told you my story to bring out two points: First, my life was a mess until I met Jesus. Then when I tried to manage my life myself, I messed it up even more. He gave me another chance and I have not turned back since. Second, when you have no skills, you need to take the initiative and do something about it to make your life better.

"Hopefully, all of you are here to better your lives. In this new age we are in, computer skills are essential for the job market. But don't forget your spiritual life. Jesus can help you through the hardships of life. He did say in the Bible, *I have come that they may have life, and that they may have it more abundantly.*"

I noticed something remarkable happened after giving my testimony; the Holy Spirit would take charge of the classroom. Also, the Christians in the class would feel emboldened to speak up for their Christian beliefs. I always felt a respect from the students and peace prevailed in the room.

Chapter Thirteen

More developments in the years 1998 to 2003.

Zuzanna wanted for many years to go to Christ For The Nations Bible School. Although she was continuously being promoted at her job, the long hours started to burn her out. So we felt this was the Lord's timing for her to take a break from her career. We moved into a three-bedroom apartment on campus at CFNI, leaving the home we were renting in Irving. Zuzanna started classes and worked part-time at Foley's.

We lived on campus for about four years. This was a good environment for the children. Joy was enrolled in the CFNI kindergarten and Gordon got involved with the youth ministry on campus. The students at the school interacted with our children often and they played with other children whose parents were students. It was a good atmosphere for our family.

Zuzanna finished the two-year CFNI regular program of classes and then decided to take a third year of Pastoral studies. She graduated in 2001 and we remained living on campus for another year.

While Zuzanna was going to school, I worked some extra jobs to make ends meet. The teaching job in West Dallas was actually only thirty hours a week so I got an evening job teaching adults computer skills in Garland. My sister was living in Rowlett then, so she even came to one of my classes in Garland.

I was still building and selling used computers. Like I said before, I wasn't making much but it provided some extra cash. Also, during this time I discovered eBay and started selling computer parts online. Many people who were building their own computers would find parts they needed on eBay. I would go to used computer auctions, buy old machines and part them out.

Asa and Gordon were going to Shady Grove Christian Academy. Our church had started a Christian school in the '80s. We felt it was important to send our children to a Christian school because the public schools had become so secular and drug-infested. Zuzanna and I felt this was the most important thing we could spend our money on—a healthy education for them. Many years we couldn't go on vacations because of this.

I think it was the summer of 2001 that we did take a "real" vacation. We had a Honda van that was well-suited for a long road trip. We started the first day by driving across Texas to Pecos, Texas, where we spent the night in a hotel. Pecos is famous for having the first rodeos. We got up the next morning and drove to Carlsbad, New Mexico, where we visited the Carlsbad Caverns. From there we went to White Sands, New Mexico, where we took off our shoes and walked across the pure white sand mounds. It was starting to get late in the afternoon and we still had many hundreds of miles to drive to Albuquerque where we had a place to stay in a CFNI friend's house. God performed a miracle on that drive up to northern New Mexico, because we went many miles with the gas gauge showing Empty. There were just no gas stations open.

When we got to Albuquerque, at two in the morning, we had to wake up a neighbor of our friend to get a key to the house. Our friend Paul was out of town but he had offered his home for us to stay. We remained there the whole next day to rest and get some sleep.

The next morning, we got up and drove up to Aztec, New Mexico, to visit a Chaco Indian village. It was really interesting to see how the Indians of northern New Mexico lived many years before the white man came. They lived in cubicles that were all joined together. Some historians believe these villages were specially designed as gathering centers for trade and special festivals for all the Indians living within a one- to two-hundred miles distance. Most of that area is semi-desert and maybe that's why they abandoned the area at some point.

We left there and traveled across northern Arizona to Flagstaff where we spent the night.

The next morning, which was the fifth day of our trip, we drove to the Grand Canyon. To me, if you only visit one national park in America, this is the one. We were driving toward the canyon, seeing signs saying, *Grand Canyon so many miles ahead*. So, we kept driving, and even entering the park at the entrance where we picked up brochures. Following the road on the brochure, we knew we were getting close but were just seeing semi-desert land. Then we saw a parking lot where some cars were parked and some people walking around. Looking at our brochure, the canyon should be right here. So, we parked and got out of the van. When we got out of the car and stood up, our breath was taken away. There it was, for miles and miles a mind-boggling canyon. We walked up closer to the rim and just stood in amazement. Fourteen miles across and one mile deep. All I could think of was *God, You are a Great Designer*.

Here I realized the difference between mountains and canyons: a mountain you can see in the distance and it gets more grandeur and defined as you get closer, but a canyon you do not see the grandeur until you get to the edge. We spent the day walking along the rim and at one point started walking down into the canyon. We were following a trail that would have led us all the way down to the Colorado River. At one point, a park ranger suggested we not go any farther because the climb back up was a health risk. I was fifty years old so she warned that I could have heart failure. Also, since we were not planning on spending the night at the bottom, they pretty much told us we had to turn around, so we did.

I don't know why but I took the bus that drove along the rim while Zuzanna and the kids stayed behind. I read in the brochure that there was a special place along the rim where when the sun was going down you could see the canyon rocks change colors. I made my way in the bus to that point and waited. Before long there must have been a hundred people that came to watch. As I sat there, I watched as the condors flew high above, looking down for animals to prey upon. (Condors are birds with the widest wingspan in the world and they are native to the Grand Canyon area.) The sun started going down and as you looked down through the canyon, sure enough, the rock walls seemed to turn colors and the shadows deepened in the crevasses. I rode the bus back to join the family and we drove back to our hotel to spend the night.

The next morning, we headed out again. In one day's time, we wanted to drive through the Painted Desert, stop at Four Corners, drive up the east side of Utah, across the Rocky Mountains and into Denver, where we were to spend a few days with an old friend and his family. We drove through the Painted Desert and were spellbound by the mesas and rock formations. On to Four Corners where we were able to stand or stretch out touching four states at once (Utah, Colorado, New Mexico and Arizona). As we drove up the east side of Utah, we went off the main highway to drive through a park where there were some stone archways. By the time we got up to Highway 70 so we could turn east toward Denver, Colorado, it was already turning dark. So, we drove across Colorado and across the Rocky Mountains in the dark. It was sad that we really didn't get to see the Rocky Mountains in daylight.

We arrived at my friend's house sometime in the early morning. It was good to see Jeff and Debbie. Their children, a boy and a girl, were younger than Asa and Gordon but older than Joy. We spent two days with them which would have been Days 6 and 7 of our trip. They took us up into a mountainous area and showed us what the old mining towns looked like.

Day 8, we got up early because we wanted to be back home in Dallas before midnight. As we drove down Colorado, we did stop at Garden of the Gods. Amazing rock formations in the park. We wished we had more time, but we had to go on. We cut across the panhandle of Texas and stopped to eat in Amarillo. We made it back home not too long after dark. It only took us twelve hours to drive from Denver to Dallas. Zuzanna drove the whole way. This was such a good trip for us as a family.

· · · · · ·

MY PARENTS

On June 22, 2002, my mother died. This was a real tragedy on many levels. She was hit by a pickup truck while crossing the road in front of my parents' house. Her cousin stopped on the other side of the road to let her out of the vehicle. As she was crossing the road, she saw a vehicle coming from one direction but did not see the pickup coming from the other direction. So, there must have been a blind spot. It was a front end impact and she died instantly. My mother's death not only impacted us as a family but shook up her community also. She was a mover and a shaker in the Dimple community, well-loved among everyone. The church was packed for her funeral.

As we gathered after the day of her death, a strange thing happened. That next day after my mother passed there was a special lunch at the community center. During the day before she died in the evening, she had cooked a few dishes so they would be ready to take the next day. So, we were sitting down to eat from the dishes my mother had cooked the previous day. I think we all had tears in our food.

There was a problem with my father. He had been diagnosed with Alzheimer's. Signs of the disease were starting to manifest. My personal opinion is that God took my mother so she would not have to see him suffer through the next four years. My father was being left helpless. Mom always did all the domestic things for him all their married lives and he would have had to go into assisted living. My sister, Glenda, decided to move from the Dallas area to take care of him. My parents owned two houses plus twenty-five acres of land.

(This land had been in my mother's family for over a hundred and eighty years. So, Glenda moved into my grandmother's old house that was vacant. Next door was my father's house, so she could take care of him. She and her husband were separated at that time so it was a doable arrangement for her.)

· · · · · ·

ODESSA, UKRAINE

In September of 2002, I took a short-term mission trip to the Ukraine. Our dear friends Wayne and Bonnie had founded a ministry, the Messianic Jewish Bible Institute, and today they have Bible Institutes for Jewish converts to Christianity all over the world. Well, their first one they planted in Odessa, Ukraine, and I was overjoyed to be able to go. (Rather than using the word Christian, they like to call themselves Completed Jews. This has to do with centuries of misguided Christians persecuting the Jewish people.)

We went to Odessa, Ukraine, to teach in the Bible school. My subject to teach was Baptisms. We were there for a week. It was an amazing trip. Not only did we teach but visited some holocaust victims. They were old by now. It was such a joy to meet them and let them know we cared. Also, we met a man that was a young boy when the Germans were rounding up the Jews in the Ukraine. He took us on a tour. We visited a monument where there had been a barn or large house. Many Jews were locked in it and then it was set on fire. Our guide was actually rescued from this barn by a Polish soldier who helped him to run off into the woods. Then he took us to a field where a hole had been dug and many children had been cast into it. Many of the children were still alive as it was covered up with dirt. He told us that for a few days the ground would move as if it was breathing. Then he took us to the Jewish cemetery, but there were no gravestones. It was a flat field with a recent erected monument identifying that it was an actual Jewish cemetery. Our guide told us that when the Russian communists came and retook Odessa, they removed all the gravestones so they could be used for road construction. We could not speak, but rather just stood in silence.

This trip to the Ukraine impacted me like no other trip I had taken. There is a back story to this that began in 1981. Often, I would go to the Dallas Public Library for research or to find interesting books. On one occasion while there, for some reason I sat down in a chair in the library to rest. On the lamp table next to me was a book someone had left there. I picked it up and noticed it was about Odessa, Ukraine. Having prayed many times for Russia and the Ukraine, it really got my attention. So, I started reading it and ended up checking it out and taking it home. As I read, God gave me a special burden for the city. I read about how it was an important port on the Black Sea and how the population was of many national origins. I dedicated myself to pray for Odessa and I placed it at the top of my prayer list. This went on for four years when I would pray for Odessa. Often, I would ask the Lord to send me there as a missionary. (As we see now, God had other plans.) So, when we went on this short-term mission trip, I was so spiritually overwhelmed just by the fact that God was fulfilling my prayers from years past. I didn't always know what to pray for during those years, but I was faithful to pray.

Intercession is an interesting thing. God burdens your heart to pray for something, but you may not be the one to fulfill it. Just be faithful to pray and then wait on the Lord to open the door for you or for someone else.

In February 2003, we moved to Grand Prairie. We bought a house about a mile from our church, Shady Grove. This was a spacious house with three bedrooms and an extra room we made into a bedroom. So, all three children had a room of their own. This was such a good house for us. Now I was close to the prayer room at church and could easily go more often.

• • • • • •

A TRIP BACK TO THE FORMER YUGOSLAVIA

In the Fall of 2003, my mother-in-law's health was at risk. I cannot remember what the risk was but she was eighty-one at that time and the family was warning that if we wanted to see her alive we should visit now. We knew we should all go, not just Zuzanna. We really did not have the money to go, but we decided that this was important and we did it anyway. So, we flew into Budapest and rented a car for the duration of our trip. My mother-in-law was so glad to see us. Asa and Gordon were in their late teens and Joy was a pre-teen. We also visited with the rest of Zuzanna's family that lived in Serbia.

Now this was eight years after the war that broke up Yugoslavia. We wanted to go to Vukovar, Croatia to visit Maria Koprivnjak. (Remember, I had worked closely with Maria in the youth camps before Zuzanna and I started dating.) In the Yugoslav war, Vukovar, situated on the border of Croatia and Serbia, had been devastated by both armies. Maria and Anton moved there to start a church a few years after the war. They took us on a tour of the city, and we saw many of the bombed-out buildings and there were bullet holes everywhere. Some of the stories they told were horrendous. The only one I will repeat here is that it took two years for the birds to feel safe enough to return to the city.

My mother-in-law went on to live another ten years. All her children came to visit her that fall and perhaps seeing everyone lifted her spirits up to live longer. This trip was so good for Asa, Gordon and Joy to be able to see their grandmother, aunts, uncles and cousins.

During her third year of CFNI, Zuzanna went back to work full-time as a manager. Full-time—I mean fifty to sixty hours a week. I gave up my second job in Garland so I could be more available for the children. Asa and Gordon were working at Six Flags amusement park, plus finishing up high school. Joy was in the 4th or 5th grade at Shady Grove Academy.

In 2004, the Housing Management company I was working for decided to close the school they were conducting for lower-income individuals. Therefore, I lost my teaching job that I loved. For the next four years, I worked some odd jobs. The main place I worked was for a fruit arrangement store called Eatable Arrangements. I delivered these beautiful baskets of fruit that were crafted to look like a flower arrangement. It was a delight showing up in offices or homes and seeing the recipients smile from ear to ear. For a while, I also worked a delivery route where I delivered ready meals to people's homes. This was a hard job. I would go to work at midnight, pack my car with sacks of food, and then drive my route. I would finish up around five a.m., find a shade tree to park and take a nap. Then, at nine a.m., show up at my Eatable Arrangements job and work about six hours. This early morning (before dawn) was really trying, but after a week or so I began to treasure the time with the Lord. I just seemed to hear Him talk to me clearly in the quietness of the city.

This was a very dark time for us as a family. I was not making much from the odd jobs and though Zuzanna was making a nice salary, it was not enough to carry the whole load. So, financially we were barely making it and most of the time we just were not making it. Looking back, these years were some of the hardest and they impacted even our children.

2008 was a year of new beginnings. Eight represents new beginnings.

I was looking on Craigslist.com for possible jobs available. There was an advertisement for a computer teacher to teach adults. I said to myself, *Oh, my gosh, this is for me.*

I called the number and got an interview. Sure enough, I got the job. I think they hired me just because I was so excited at the possibility of getting back to doing what I liked. So, I went to work for the Wilkenson Center, a nonprofit, in East Dallas. They let me use the curriculum I had developed at the previous place I worked. To me, this was not work but something I truly enjoyed. Someone said,

"If you enjoy your job, you will never work a day in your life." They almost had to force me to take vacations.

By this time Asa and Gordon were out of high school and there were a couple of years where I home-schooled Joy. Asa had joined the Army Reserves and Gordon was working at Six Flags amusement park in Arlington, Texas. Asa had already been deployed to Iraq and may have already returned.

· · · · · ·

MISSION TRIP TO SERBIA

In the summer of 2008, two friends, Norvel and Eva Rohrer, and I went on a mission trip to Serbia. We connected with Viktor Sabo's church where Norvel and Eva taught and I preached. Norvel and I also preached in some of the village churches.

While in Subotica in 2008, I did something really dumb, even though my motive was good. Viktor pointed out to me that the old Yugoslav Army Camp in Subotica was abandoned. I knew of this camp very well because the Bartok Bela church where I had served in the '80s was just a block away and you had to walk past it often. When Serbia made peace with NATO troops, part of the agreement was that they had to move all military bases and equipment away from the borders. Viktor talked about how there were all these buildings sitting unoccupied and they had a vision to use them to house a drug-addict program or houses for the poor. So, I told Viktor I would go do a prayer-walk around the complex. Now the complex is large, a good thirty acres, with all kinds of buildings for barracks, offices, kitchens, warehouses, etc.

One day I went to the camp for the purpose of prayer-walking around it. Well, the camp has a ten-foot wall all the way around it. So, I started my prayer-walk, walking around the outside of the wall, praying in the spirit, declaring that wherever my foot treads it shall be claimed for the Lord. I got to the back side of the camp, where the gate is, and noticed the gate was open. I decided to step inside the compound. There were no cars around and no sign of any guards. So, I just kept stepping. I thought to myself, *well, maybe I am to prayer-walk the inside of this camp.* I went from building to building, across the drill field, peeked into the windows, and saw the four-story barracks. I noticed the barracks were rather newly built and would be excellent quarters for working with addicts.

Then I got to a warehouse and when I looked in through the big sliding doors I saw about ten fully armored tanks parked. I remembered how Viktor had talked about how all the cannons and tanks had to be moved farther from the border, back into the interior of the country, so this here was in violation of the NATO agreement. I realized I really, *really* should not be there. Okay, let me head toward the gate and get out of here. But when I got near the gate, I heard men talking. I also noticed a car parked at the gate. So, I sat down behind a bush, and started contemplating how I could be in real trouble if I was found out.

Oh, Lord, get me out of this situation.

After about fifteen minutes, the men got in the car and left. I was so relieved. All right, let me get out of here while I can. I went up to the gate, but it was now locked. Oh wow, I am now locked inside. I looked around and found a place to climb over the wall.

I told Viktor what had happened and showed him pictures I had taken. Once back in the U.S., I shared it with Zuzanna and she really got on my case, realizing her husband could have been in jail. I don't know what will happen in the future, but that camp has been claimed for the Lord.

I began to set aside my mornings unto the Lord. At least once or twice a week I would go to the prayer room at church and spend thirty minutes to an hour with the Lord. Some days the Lord would tell me to go to a place in the metroplex and pray: like city hall, to pray for government, or a courthouse to pray for justice, etc. Sometimes

I would go by Christ For The Nations and attend their eight a.m. worship time. It was such a great way to prepare for the day. I began to look for some others to pray with in the mornings. There is just more power in corporate prayer. Jesus said, "Where two or three are gathered, He is in our midst."

I couldn't find anyone at my church available in the morning hours and I was sad. I prayed God would direct me to a prayer group that met early mornings. For a while I would drop by a ministry in South Dallas where they ministered to drug addicts and street people. It was not a circle of prayer but rather more a time of prayer for their ministry.

· · · · · ·

UPPERROOM

I think it was 2010 and 2011 that I joined a weekly meeting in West Dallas. This was a home group-type meeting where personal needs were met around fellowship. It was led by two seasoned guys named Randy and Ron. There was also an anointed worship leader named Bob. The group was dissolved or either I could no longer go. I did really enjoy the group and Zuzanna came with me a few times.

Sometime in the spring I got an email from Bob that he was leading worship at a new church in the Oak Lawn area. My first thought was, *Can anything good come out of Oak Lawn?*

Oak Lawn was considered the homosexual area of Dallas. I decided to check out their website. So, I found the website for UPPERROOM. The amazing thing I noticed was that they were mainly a house of prayer and they had early-morning prayer at 6:00 a.m. three days a week. I located the address of UPPERROOM and realized it was along my way to work. I also noticed they had a prayer set on Saturday mornings from 10 to 12 noon, so then I decided to go on a Saturday to check it out. The first time I went I thought I'd never find it. Finally, I found the stairway leading up to the entrance. Sure enough, it was an upper room above a veterinarian clinic. I walked in and there was a band playing and about twelve people scattered around the room. It was much like the ANHOP prayer room I had attended before at my church. I took my place and spent time with the Lord. At the end, everyone gathered for a short corporate prayer time together. As I started to leave, a young lady named Hannah introduced herself and asked if she could pray for me. I definitely felt the Spirit of the Lord in the place.

The next week I decided to drop in at 6 a.m. on the way to work. When I got there, I noticed there was not a band leading worship but rather off in a corner a group of about eight people. I walked over and everyone looked up at me, I guess because they had not seen me before.

I asked, "Ya'll pray here?"

They said yes, and invited me to sit down. That day in June 2011 started two-and-a-half years of once or twice a week prayer time for me in the prayer room. I got to know these early-morning prayer warriors, and many are still close friends. The weekly prayer times were different than the Saturday set. They were more of a circle with one person with a guitar leading worship. Later on, it would grow to where they had a full band in these morning prayer times. In those days, UPPERROOM had prayer three times a day: morning, noon and night. I found there a real eagerness in the people to pray and spend time with the Lord. It was so good to enjoy the presence of the Lord with others.

A few weeks after I started going to these prayer sets, I decided to attend a Sunday afternoon service. The only time they had a church service was on Sunday at 5 p.m. I arrived and the room was packed. Most of the people were in their twenties and thirties. The service was a full, get-excited-about-Jesus, charismatic-type worship. I really felt at home. I went home really lit up. Zuzanna was working that day, but when she got home, I was so excited to tell her about my experience at UPPERROOM we both went the following Sunday. We still loved attending our regular church, Shady Grove, on Sunday mornings but Sunday evenings we went to UPPERROOM.

· · · · · ·

THE GYPSIES OF ROMANIA

Let me back up to 2010. In the winter a man who was a part of Shady Grove Church for many years and a former elder approached me about taking a short-term trip with him and a team of people to Romania. Jeff had moved to Europe and started an outreach ministry to Europe. European Initiative was mainly a street ministry that took teams and did skits in European plazas, drew a crowd, and shared Jesus. They would see many get saved and healed. EIs ministry trips to Romania were a little different. They would go into Gypsy villages, go house to house handing out coats, shoes, food, etc., and then share the Gospel with the household. The next trip was planned for January 2011. I told Jeff I would pray about it. I talked it over with Zuzanna and we decided I should go.

Earlier that same year (2010), a friend of ours had given us a word from the Lord that in three years we would be living in the Balkans. Our friend, Elias, at that time was the head of missions at Shady Grove Church. We had been praying about moving back to the Balkans to do ministry someday but now we were tied down with a mortgage and car loans. I still felt trapped in America. There *was* a ray of hope—we realized Joy, our youngest, would graduate from high school in three years.

Little did I know how much this trip would impact me and eventually Zuzanna also.

January was the coldest time of the year in Romania and Jeff said to be sure I had layers of clothes and a thick coat for this remote area we were going to. I packed up and flew into Bucharest, Romania, a day early before the other members of the team flew in. I came a day early because I wanted to do a prophetic prayer-walk around the capitol building of the country. I had read up on the building which the former dictator Nicolae Ceaușescu built. He had wiped out a large area of Bucharest, uprooting people from their ancestral homes, squeezing money from other cities in the country just to build this massive government building and decorative streets and apartments. The capitol building at the time was the second-largest building in the world. So, I took the next day to go to the capitol and did the prayer-walk. I had planned to go around three times but I realized it was four miles around the building and the surrounding grounds so I only walked around it once. That evening the team flew in.

The next morning, one of the pastors from Apata, the city we were going to, met us at the hotel and we packed his van and another van we rented. Matt led the team because Jeff was sick and could not come. We headed out to a department store (much like a Target or Walmart in America) where we bought coats, gloves, hats and food. There were about ten of us on the team so we entered, each getting a cart, and just started filling them up.

I was shocked at the abundance of available items. I remember when I was in Romania in the '80s, around the last years of communism, there was almost nothing in the stores. If you know anyone who believes in communism, let me talk to them. Communism is brutal on its citizens. Romania got their freedom in the winter of 1989.

We bought everything, packed up the vans, and started toward Apata. Oh, now I remember, we also had rented a car. I rode with the pastor in his van. A God thing happened as we started driving over the mountains. The pastor told me we were entering the area of Romania called Transylvania. The Holy Spirit hit me and I just began to weep. I don't know if I was thinking of the demonic writings over the centuries about Transylvania or what but I was groaning in intercession. We drove on to Apata and found our hotel. Snow was about a foot deep. The next morning, we met at the church where we met the Romanian and Gypsy locals. We also met Pastor Edward, the senior pastor. We had a time of prayer and worship and then set up tables so we could sort the clothing. The prayer time was really powerful; a strong wind hit the building, shaking the windows, and blew open the door. One of the Roma (Gypsy) and I went outside, and we felt the wind ceasing and returning to no wind at all. We both looked at each other knowing this was the Lord's wind. I think it was the anointing of the Lord coming upon us.

We had four days of going to four villages where we went house to house sharing Jesus and giving out coats, gloves, shoes, etc. We foreigners teamed up with one or two Roma that also knew English and could translate for us. We would first explain the Gospel and hopefully lead them in a prayer of salvation. Then we would take the family's sizes and then send a runner to our van to get the clothing gifts. How many of these people were truly giving their life to the Lord, we don't know. It is likely some did pray the prayer just to get the gifts, although that was not a requirement. Only God knows. There is something I always try to do with those I lead to the Lord: I have them tell someone else that they have accepted Jesus. The Bible says to confess Him before others and you will be saved.

Overall, I prayed with thirty-four people to receive Jesus. This just blew me away. I felt so good. It was as if the Lord was saying, "See how I can use you when you step out for me." It was as if I had gone to a new spiritual level.

I came back to Texas so happy that I had decided to go on that trip to Romania. I will forever be grateful to European Initiative and Jeff for asking me to go on this trip. Zuzanna noticed a big change in me and how this trip had lit me up.

I went back to my job and continued to go to early-morning prayer at UPPERROOM. This trip to Romania was an annual trip that EI did each January so the 2012 trip was being planned. I talked with Zuzanna about going on this next trip. We looked at our finances and decided she could go. We told EI that we had the money for one of us to go and that Zuzanna would be the one to go. EI then stepped up and offered to pay for me to go also. So, we both went on the 2012 trip. We went to the Apata area of Romania and basically did the same thing we had done before.

......

IS THIS THE TIME, LORD?

On this 2012 trip, Jeff asked Zuzanna and me to pray about becoming a part of European Initiative. Since we were burdened for the Balkans and Zuzanna was fluent in the Serbian and Croatian language, Jeff suggested we start an EI base somewhere in the Balkans. We felt this was what God was speaking to us and we decided to talk to the elders at Shady Grove about sending us out. We remembered the word Elias, the mission's director, gave us in 2010; that we would be living in the Balkans in three years. So, we were feeling more and more that 2012 would be our last year in the States and we should start preparations for a move to the Balkans.

The elders at Shady Grove Church also felt this was God's timing for us and said they would raise money during the annual October Mission's Conference to send us out. When the conference came about, a set amount was raised for us. We then started the process of raising the rest of the funds needed. In September of 2013 we hit a plateau at about 50 percent of the needed funds. European Initiative told us that we would need at least 80 percent before they would let us relocate. This was a good safety measure so that we would not go prematurely and get stranded overseas with no funds. We continued contacting friends and having home gatherings to share our vision.

Let me step back to 2011 and talk about a blessing we had. For a few years, Zuzanna had a special savings fund preparing for our twenty-fifth wedding anniversary. We wanted to go on a cruise. We decided the best cruise would be in the Mediterranean, and we would combine it with a trip to Subotica, Serbia, to see Zuzanna's family. We first flew into Rome, got bed- and-breakfast accommodations near the airport, and easy access to the rail/subway system. We spent three days in Rome where we toured the city. We bought on-off tickets for a tour bus that covered most of the city.

First, we went to the Colosseum. As we toured the Colosseum, I reflected deeply, realizing the blood of the martyrs shed that paved the way for the spread of Christianity. Just to think what they had to go through so I could enjoy my freedom to worship Jesus now. We toured the Vatican and many other places in Rome also.

On the fourth day of our vacation, we went aboard the cruise ship. Oh, by the way, it was Gordon, Joy, Zuzanna and I on this trip. Asa was still in the military and was deployed to Afghanistan. He could not get leave to join us so we were sad that he was not with us.

We sailed from Italy to Messina, Sicily. Joy, Zuzanna and I walked around Messina while Gordon stayed in the cabin to catch up on sleep as he had worked many hours so he could take this time off. We visited an old church where at noon each day there is a special event in the belfry where the striking of the noon bell is a display of many moving figures, one of the figures being a lion that strikes the bell.

The ship left Messina in the late evening and sailed all night to Athens, Greece. So the next morning we took a tour of the Acropolis. Before going to the Acropolis, we stopped at the stadium where the first modern Olympics were held in 1896. Then on to the Acropolis where we walked among the ancient buildings of Athens that have been there for thousands of years. From the Acropolis you can look out in all directions across the city.

The next night, we sailed over to the coast of Turkey where we could tour Ephesus. Ephesus is all in ruins now but it was amazing to tour what was once the third-largest city in the Roman Empire and where the largest church was during the days of the Apostles John, Paul, et al.

From Ephesus we sailed down to Crete where the next day we spent some time on a beach. The next night, we sailed from Crete to our original Italian port and that concluded our cruise. We went from the ship directly to the airport.

When we got to the airport, I noticed my wallet was missing. Then I remembered how at the train station when walking back to the train boarding platform a man ran past me, as though he was in a hurry, and had bumped into me. He must have quickly reached into my back pocket and grabbed my wallet. There was about $350 in cash, and now I had to try and connect with my bank and get my credit/debit card cancelled. The biggest loss to me was my original social security card that had written on it, "Not to be used for Identification," which we know to be a joke now.

We went on to Serbia to visit Zuzanna's family and then on to Budapest, Hungary.

Chapter Fourteen

2013 began with another trip to Romania. This year, Zuzanna was put in charge of organizing the trip. There was a charity organization that contacted us about a container of over four thousand boots that they had to donate. The Crocs Company donated them to a charity and they were looking for a worthy cause to give it to. European Initiative decided to take on the project and distribute these boots on the Romanian outreach. This was not an easy task for Zuzanna, but her Logistics experience at Target was great preparation. I was amazed at how she pulled off this amazing feat of getting these shoes from America to Romania amidst great challenges all along the way.

At the same time, she was still the Store Manager at Old Navy, managing Christmas season. There were so many roadblocks that had to be overcome. Getting the shipment to Romania on time, getting the shoes through Romanian customs, and then having them shipped across Romania in the winter. There were so many miracles that happened to get these shoes to the outreach point. The outreach point was Apata again. The good thing about Apata was the fact that there was a church there to follow up after we left.

On this particular outreach, we went house to house giving out tickets to residents so they could attend a meeting in the afternoon. During the meeting, we shared Jesus, prayed with many to receive Jesus, and then passed out shoes. We did this in three villages and in the city of Apata. The distribution went smoothly in the villages but in Apata we had a problem. We had given out about eight hundred tickets to the gypsy community. The people came and the community building we rented was full. Many people gathered outside who had heard of the distribution but did not receive tickets. The Gospel was preached and many received Jesus. Then we had it set up so that as they exited, we would fit them with shoes. It was going okay until a large crowd formed at the entrance wanting also to get in and get shoes. They were pressing up against the entrance and the people exiting could not get out.

The main challenge Zuzanna was facing was that in Romania public buildings are not required to have two separate entrance/exit doors. Additionally, we found out that our local contacts did not disclose the size of the event to the police department, who would have provided adequate oversight had they known. Inside the building there began to be a real concern with the people being able to get out. Finally, police showed up to come and disperse the crowds. Although around eight hundred people heard the Gospel, and many boots were distributed, the event did not end well. Nevertheless, we learned a lot from that experience.

When Zuzanna and I left Romania, we flew to Zagreb. After joining European Initiative, we needed to find a location in the Balkans to open a base. EI asked that it be in a capital city. The considerations were Bucharest, Belgrade and Zagreb. I was personally favoring Belgrade. Zuzanna felt a leaning to Zagreb. Then an old friend of ours who lived in Croatia suggested that we could rent a furnished apartment in the Evangelical Pentecostal Churches (EPC) headquarters building. We felt that this was a sign that Zagreb may actually be where God wanted us because I had once spent the night in that building back in 1984. So, we decided to go check it out before flying back to Texas. We spent four days in Zagreb checking out the apartment and the city. We then flew back to the States with a goal of raising the support we needed to make the move.

We continued our jobs, Zuzanna at Old Navy and I at the Wilkenson Center. As I was already retired, but still working part-time, the rest of our time we were meeting with anyone interested to hear about our vision and heart for the Balkans. We are most thankful for those early supporters like Bill and Molly, Truman and Jane, and the Generations Church in Granbury, Texas.

· · · · · · ·

REALIGNMENT

I believe it was in February 2012 that Shady Grove became part of Gateway Church in Southlake, Texas. The pastor of Gateway had been an elder at Shady Grove at one time and it was an agreeable arrangement by most of the Shady Grove members. Because of the close relationship between the churches, it was a win-win merger. Anytime this sort of thing happens, tough decisions must be made, and so it was that individual missionaries would no longer be supported by the church. This affected us personally as we counted on Shady Grove to be our sending church.

The reality of this merger was quite a shock. Zuzanna and I were asking the Lord what this meant to us personally? Here we were, preparing to re-launch to the mission field, and the church we called home for many decades was no more. We could not launch without a spiritual covering. What are you saying to us, God?

I personally really believed in the prayer-first concept and UPPERROOM excelled in that aspect. We slowly reduced our attendance at Gateway Grand Prairie (the new name of the old Shady Grove campus) and gave ourselves totally to UPPERROOM. Our gut-feeling was that UPPERROOM was taking our understanding of worship and the Tabernacle of David to a higher level.

Now there was something that really helped me through this transition. I was thumbing through Mike Bickle's lessons at this time and came across a teaching on "moves of God." He talked about how a move-of-God usually lasts from thirty to forty years. Then it will take different forms according to how it is managed. The move-of-God either implodes with false hope of the return of past glory or it comes into its divine purpose in the sphere where it is planted. I had actually seen both happen to churches in the Dallas metroplex I had either been a part of or knew about.

The part of Mike Bickle's teaching that really satisfied my question was how he described the real purpose of a move-of-God. God seemed to always use it to select out those He had destined to lead the next move-of-God. I knew this is what had happened at Shady Grove. I saw the destinies of many come to maturity and could identify these people coming into their divine purpose. There is no doubt in my mind that Gateway Church grew out of the forty-year move-of-God that Shady Grove championed. Also, I knew UPPERROOM was a move-of-God that was in its early stages and God clearly told Zuzanna and me that this was where He wanted us.

Now remember, we hit a financial plateau in the summer. God opened an opportunity to share our vision and plans with Michael, the founding pastor of UPPERROOM. Michael got pretty excited and wanted us to share about it at the next Sunday night and they then took up an offering. This was a huge boost and got us up to nearly 70 percent! Little by little, commitments started coming in again. Finally, during the fall of 2013, UPPERROOM commissioned us to be sent out to the mission field.

About this time (September 2013), I had a dream. I dreamed that we were living in Zagreb in the apartment we were to rent. Here is the dream: I woke up in the morning in that apartment and looked out the window. It was snowing, so I woke Zuzanna and told her, "Look, here is the first snowfall this winter."

The interpretation the Lord gave us was that we would be living in that apartment before the first snowfall in Zagreb. This gave us reassurance that we would meet the finances needed/required for making the move. Sure enough, funds started coming in and by the first of November we reached our goal. We started packing and bought airline tickets for December. It was decided Zuzanna would fly on December 14 and I would wait until December 28. This was designed so she could start setting up the apartment in Zagreb and she could go to Serbia and spend Christmas with her mother and family there. I still had things concerning our house in Grand Prairie that needed to be wrapped up, plus I would then spend Christmas with Joy. At this time, Gordon was traveling with the Ringling Brothers Circus and Asa was living in Utah.

As far as taking care of the house, it was being sold and its contents had to be eliminated. We had several garage sales, online sales and we donated what was left to charity. I would say we liquidated 90 percent of what we owned. Family keepsakes and personal valuables were stored in East Texas at my grandmother's old house. When my father passed, we inherited half of my parents' land, along with the old house of my grandmother's. Twice we tried renting it out but that never worked well. Finally, I sold the house and an acre and two-thirds to my cousin Cindy. She had grown up in the house, so it meant a lot to her. We still retain 11.5 acres of the original land.

PART FIVE

BACK TO A DREAM

Chapter Fifteen

We were Croatia-bound. Zuzanna arrived on December 14, 2013. She bought some things for our new apartment and then took a bus to her mother's house in Serbia. After being there a few days, a tragic but glorious thing happened—Ester Balint died and passed into heaven. She was ninety-one years old, and the medic just said she tired-out and her heart stopped. She had gotten up from the table and was unsteady. Zuzanna came over to hold her up and Ester collapsed in Zuzanna's arms. She was an amazing woman, having given birth to eleven children and managed a home through wars and peace. Although I could not talk with her, I loved her so much.

By the time I flew into Croatia, Zuzanna had returned to Zagreb. We began setting up the Balkan base for European Initiative and settling into our new life. The second week of January, we flew from Zagreb to Cluj, Romania, and went on to Targu Mures, where the 2014 EI Romanian outreach was to happen.

But now there was a new problem: I was very sick. My lungs were full of fluid and I had a deep cough. This started almost as soon as I landed in Croatia. I thought that by the time I got to Romania I would be over it. Zuzanna and I had gone to Targu Mures two days early so Zuzanna could take care of any last-minute arrangements for the outreach. When Jeff and the rest of the team got there it was decided I needed to go to the hospital to be checked out.

Daci, our contact in Targu Mures, made arrangements for an examination for me at a hospital. They did some tests and determined I had bronchial pneumonia. I was confined to our hotel room and could not participate in the outreach. Twice a day, a nurse came to the hotel room to give me a shot of antibiotics and steroids. Then the outreach was over and we flew back to Croatia. The antibiotics helped some but when I got back in Croatia it started hitting me again. We went to a hospital near where we lived and they examined me and came up with the same diagnosis, pneumonia. More antibiotics were given to me. After more doctor's visits, lots of coughing, and little sleep, we were running out of options. Because we had just arrived in the country and still were in the process of obtaining our visas, we could not have insurance, and due to EU regulations, "third-country citizens" (outside of the EU) had limited options. We were praying hard and asked everyone we knew to pray. Finally, I got to a point where I could not sleep. I would doze off and quickly wake up gasping for air. I had gone two days without sleep.

Now, Zuzanna had a meeting with two ladies concerning ministry to the gypsies in Croatia. We had determined that when she got back, we would go back to the hospital. At the end of the meeting, Zuzanna shared with the two ladies my situation. One of the ladies said, "My roommate is a nurse." So they called her and she made arrangements for me to be taken to the emergency room of her hospital the next morning. This meant I would have to make it through the night, waiting until morning. I know this was the worst night I have ever spent in my life. It basically meant I needed to stay awake all night just to keep from suffocating. I could not lie down.

I was really scared and wanted to call my children to say goodbye. I felt I would not make it till morning. Zuzanna said I was doing no such thing. Finally, the morning came and the nurse came to pick us up. Once at the emergency room, they assigned a doctor to me that said, "We are throwing out all prior diagnosis and doing our own test." This was music to our ears as each place we had been to added confusion to the mix.

By the way, the name of the hospital was Holy Spirit, Sveti Duh in Croatian.

After a few tests, it was determined I did not have pneumonia, but instead was diagnosed with congestive heart failure. Somehow my heart was not pumping the fluid off of my lungs. (That is my description, not a medical description.) They went on to find that one side of my heart was enlarged and was causing congestive heart failure. The first thing they did was stick a large needle through my back into my right lung and pumped out a liter of fluid. They did this mainly so I could get some sleep. I was put in a room with three or four other men. I slept some; not sure how long but when I woke up they drained my right lung once again. At some point, I was hooked up to oxygen.

I stayed in the hospital for about four days. I saw a heart specialist in the hospital, and he prescribed the medications I needed for my heart. He informed us of the good and bad news. First there was no real surgery that could fix my heart. Once it is enlarged, it does not shrink back to a normal size. I would need to take medication for the rest of my life. I could die at any time or live ten years or so. I needed to take it easy because I would remain very weak and had to stay on a strict diet.

After returning from the hospital, I spent about two weeks asking God "Why me, why now?" We had prayed for years to be able to return to the Balkans for ministry and now this heart disease. Finally, I just promised the Lord I would serve Him as much as I could with my physical weakness. We did not have a car at that time, so we had to walk or take public transportation. I stayed home most of the time, or if I did get out, I often had to stop and sit down to rest.

Part of our job with European Initiative was to make contact with local pastors so they could help us and we help them with ministry teams. A big part of EIs strategy for local ministry was to include local churches to provide translators, housing and follow-up. So, we met with many of the pastors in Zagreb and beyond. Most were willing to meet with us. Often, we would visit their church first and then set up a meeting. Some of the pastors wanted us to come preach in their church. We did preach in a few but we let them know we were there mainly to support them as pastors, seeking ways to be of help. Because of my heart condition, they pledged to pray for me, and we let them know we were praying for them and their churches.

Zuzanna was the organizer. She mainly had the responsibility to organize the EI outreaches in the Balkans. One of the events we started working on for Zagreb was to bring Ballet Magnificat! to the city. If you are not familiar with Ballet Magnificat!, they are a professional Christian ballet company. The whole company and support staff equaled sixteen, so housing, meals, transportation and the events had to be arranged.

It was arranged for them to perform on the main square in Zagreb, Ban Jelacic, and at one of the shopping malls. They performed a ballet story and then one or two of the ballet dancers would give their testimony of how they met Jesus. Many pedestrians gathered to watch and then the dancers, along with translators, would disperse into the crowd to witness to the onlookers. We witnessed to many people and there were some who gave their lives to Jesus. We tried to take note of their personal information so the churches could follow up. It was encouraging to see some of the local pastors come out to help us as well.

As we were making contact with local churches, we connected with a group called Borongajci. This group was named after an area of Zagreb where there had been a revival just after the Yugoslav war in the '90s. They were more of an organic group that mainly met on Saturdays. Zuzanna and I attended a few meetings and got to meet some of the people. They mainly met as small groups and then once a month they would meet all together. Some of their small groups were rather large by Croatian standards for churches.

· · · · · ·

WE DON'T SEE THIS HERE...HE HAS A PERFECTLY HEALTHY HEART

In July 2014, the leadership of Borongajci decided to have a prayer meeting on a mountain in Lika. Lika is a region or municipal county in the center of Croatia. We were not sure exactly why it was organized but it was a prayer meeting and we wanted to be a part of it. We didn't ask many questions, especially as to what type of terrain we were going to. We thought we would drive up the side of a mountain, there would be a park, and we would assemble to have prayer and worship. Well, we arrived at the base of a mountain and then had to climb up a trail that wound around up the mountain. I went a little ways, but just could not go any farther. I went back to the car to wait and pray on my own.

This mountain is unique in that it has a somewhat flat surface near the top. They actually managed to get musical instruments and a sound system up there. At times, if the wind was just right, I could hear the sound from below, especially when they blew the shofars. Then the unimaginable happened: the biggest storm I have ever seen in Croatia blew in. It was soaking rain with lightning and thunder. I grew up with these kinds of storms in Texas but had never seen anything like this in the Balkans. The people were scrambling down the mountain as fast as they could. I am convinced this was the devil striking back. As an intercessor, I understand the enemy had a stronghold on the country and was not going down lightly. I found out later that this mountain was a main lookout and communication point during many wars over the centuries. Also, witch covens have used the mountain for black arts. But God's people went and prayed, planted a Christian flag, and made the devil mad as hell.

Zuzanna and I drove back to Zagreb and in the next week I noticed my strength returning. I could walk longer distances without having to stop and rest. Our apartment was on the third floor and I could climb the stairs all the way up without stopping halfway to rest. I told Zuzanna, "I am healed. I should stop taking the heart medicine."

She said, "No way!" and reminded me I had a checkup scheduled with the heart doctor in two weeks.

So, in two weeks we went to the heart doctor handling my case. First, we had to go have an ultrasound done at another clinic so we could present the results to the doctor. That scan showed that my heart looked good but that the heart specialist would have to fully analyze the findings. We showed up to my heart doctor for his examination. He did not talk much but he sure had a questioning look on his face. He had an ultrasound machine in his office and decided to take his own ultrasound. I thought he was going to press that sensor through my ribs as he went back and forth across my heart area. Finally, he sat down at his desk and scanned through all my blood work and tests. Then he sat back in his chair and said in his broken English, "We don't see this here."

Zuzanna said, "What do you mean?"

"We don't see this here. He has a perfectly healthy heart."

Zuzanna asked, "Can you say that again?"

The doctor repeated, "He has a perfectly formed heart. It is back to its normal size."

We asked, "What does that mean?"

"I am taking you off the medication and you can go live a normal life with a normal heart."

When he had first diagnosed me with congestive heart failure and the fact that my life was at high risk, I told him I had many people praying for me. He ignored my comment. I just wish I had taken that last time in his office to really proclaim the healing power of Jesus.

Zuzanna and I left his office in silence. We were really struck by the reality of a divine miracle. This was a real testimony to the pastors, churches in Croatia, our supporters in the States, and our family.

John 9:1 Now as Jesus passed by, He saw a man who was blind from birth. 2 And His disciples asked Him, saying, "Rabbi, who sinned, this man or his parents, that he was born blind?" ³ Jesus answered, "Neither this man nor his parents sinned, but that the works of God should be revealed in him."

I am just so grateful Jesus passed by.

∙ ∙ ∙ ∙ ∙ ∙

OTHER THINGS THAT HAPPENED THAT FIRST YEAR IN CROATIA

We made a trip to Kosovo to attend a meeting of Balkan Networks. I had connected with Balkan Networks a few years earlier from the States by email. Balkan Networks is a group of like-minded pastors and ministry leaders in the Balkans. They meet once or twice a year to encourage each other and collectively pray about what God is doing in the Balkan countries.

As part of my efforts to pray and recruit others to pray for the Balkans, I had connected with this group. Zuzanna and I looked forward to this meeting. Also, we had made contact with a ministry in Montenegro that ministered among the gypsies there so we decided we would make visiting them a part of this trip.

We rented a car and drove the first day all the way down the Croatian coast into Montenegro and got a hotel room. Our trip down the coast was amazing as we discovered how beautiful it was. The next morning in Montenegro we met with our contact and went to visit the gypsy sector. This was an area of Podgorica, the capital of Montenegro, where a refugee camp had been set up for those gypsies that had to flee Kosovo during the Serbia/Kosovo war of 1999. They had been in this camp for many years now with very little chance of moving on. Their situation was that most of them had no identity in regard to citizenship or a paper trail.

Sinisa, our contact there, was trained as a lawyer and had been doing what he could to help them establish an identity so they could immigrate to other countries. The Montenegrin government didn't want to make them citizens so they were caught in a Catch 22 situation. What identity they did have was locked up in Belgrade, Serbia, which did not want to cooperate with any Kosovars.

Sinisa had started a church in the camp. Now these Kosovar gypsies had an Islamic background. We were amazed at how Sinisa would use sayings from the Koran to back up biblical principles. This was hard for Zuzanna and me to wrap our minds around, but we could not deny the fruits.

This camp was built near the city dump. Mainly these people made a living scavenging from the dump. They would dig through the trash trying to find metal they could sell to recyclers.

We had a problem with going from Montenegro to Kosovo. The car we had rented could not be driven into Kosovo because rental companies thought it unsafe to drive their vehicles there. We left the car with Sinisa in Montenegro and we took a bus to Kosovo. Although we had to still pay for the car rental while it sat in Montenegro, this was cheaper than having to pay the rental company to drive it back to Zagreb and then for us to rent another car for the trip back home. So, the next morning we caught a bus in Podgorica that took us across the mountains to Gjakova, Kosovo. It took all day because the road was pretty harsh and winding.

It was an awesome three-day meeting which initiated and enhanced future relationships with some movers-and-shakers in the Balkans. We got to meet face-to-face with some of the men and women I had been emailing for a few years now: Dag from Albania, Bryan from Macedonia, George from Greece, Filip from Bulgaria, Lee from Romania, Kati from Albania, Venco from Macedonia, Mike from Greece, and many others.

Mike had brought four men with him that were visiting his ministry. They were from Argentina. There were two young men and two older men. We expected that one of the older men was the leader of this group, but were astonished to discover that Yonathan, a

19-year-old, was their lead man. We came to find out that his father in Argentina was an Apostolic leader of over eight hundred churches. Yonathan grew up in the revivals in Argentina over the past twenty years. There was a maturity in this young man that truly astounded us. He spoke with great wisdom and spiritual authority. They spoke of their plans to mobilize hundreds of missionaries from South America to take the Gospel back to Europe as a way of thanking Europe for bringing the Gospel to them many years ago.

After the meeting concluded, we took the bus back through the mountains of Kosovo and Montenegro to Podgorica. We spent the night there and spent the next day driving back up the coast to Zagreb. Once again, we drove by the beautiful coast but did not have time to stop and enjoy it.

Back in Zagreb, we continued to meet with pastors and attend their churches. We found ourselves drawn more and more to the Borongajci group. I found out that they had a prayer meeting every weekday morning at 6 a.m. So, I started attending once or twice a week. I would get up around 5 a.m., catch the bus and trams and be at the prayer meeting by a little after 6 a.m.

I got to know Saša, Tomislav, and Marko who were taking turns leading the early-morning prayer. As I have learned, every prayer group is different. Mainly we would talk a lot of spiritual matters and then spend thirty minutes or more in prayer at the end. Very few people showed up for this prayer time, but it was usually intercessory prayer and was powerful.

Another thing happened in the summer of 2014. Joy came to visit and brought our dog, Hershey. It was a joy to now have him with us. He was left behind when I couldn't get him on the flight initially, due to complications with the airlines.

I am not sure of the exact dates but Yonathan, his girlfriend Miru, and an Argentinian pastor came to visit Zagreb. Yonathan was the young man we met at the Balkan Networks meeting in Kosovo. We needed to schedule a venue for Yonathan to address so we contacted the pastor of the largest Protestant church in Croatia. He was eager to have Yonathan hold revival meetings at his church. We found an excellent Spanish translator and the meetings began.

I'm not sure how many evenings there were, but one of the evenings was outstanding. The worship was amazing. I knelt down with my face on the floor. God began to give me a vision. It was a mental vision, not an open vision. (I have not had many visions in my life and only once an open vision.) The Lord began to show me that we were running across a bridge, with our hands raised in worship. The land behind us was dark but the land ahead of us was bright as if it was heaven. (We, in this vision, were the people in this meeting.) Then I looked down, and I noticed the bridge was made out of bones—human bones. I asked the Lord, "Why bones?" He had me look back at the dark land we were running from and I saw a passing of time in that land. I saw men and women praying. Then the Lord began to interpret the vision to me, "The bridge you are crossing from darkness into light was built by the prayers of those praying saints. For many years, over the centuries, many people had prayed to see the day when revival would come to Croatia. They prayed but they did not see it. But I took their bones and built this bridge so you could now come to victory."

Even to this day I remember that vision and I am drawn to respect those that went before us so we could enjoy the blessings of God.

There were other outreaches throughout the year. In the fall of 2014, Zuzanna planned an outreach with Church of the Highlands, to Hungary and Romania. This was a very unforgettable trip for this team. We met a really awesome group of people we got to know really well. Over the next few years, we made trips to Birmingham, Alabama, to visit with them and attend conferences at their church. At the end of this trip, we were to visit Zuzanna's sister Hajnalka in Serbia. Their mother had passed a year earlier, and Zuzanna wanted to be with her sister on that day.

· · · · · ·

"IT IS TIME TO RUN WITH YOUR OWN VISION"

On our drive from Budapest to Subotica, we discussed our first year on the mission field. We both realized there was an unsettling feeling about it. We knew that EI was satisfied with the results, but somehow, we were not. We realized that though what we were doing served the Kingdom, we felt that we were not walking in our calling. We really did not know what to do with this realization, but we both stated it and brought it before the Lord.

In January of 2015, Zuzanna planned another multi-country outreach, this time for Charis Bible College. The team was to go to Croatia, Hungary, and then European Initiative's annual January Romanian outreach.

On the way back from Targu Mures, the city of the Romania outreach, we wanted to visit Lee Saville's ministry near Arad, Romania. Lee was a part of the Balkan Networks whom we met in Kosovo and we wanted to get to know him and visit his ministry. We took a train and got there in the early evening, so we met him at our hotel for dinner.

Shortly after we sat down, he said, "Before we get to talking and sharing, I believe I have a word for you. Let me give it and you can judge it. I feel the Lord wants to tell you that you have served another man's vision and now it is time to run with your own vision."

As I alluded to it above, Zuzanna and I had already been questioning if we really fit into European Initiative. There was more to the word, too, that confirmed some things in our hearts. This word Lee gave us had such authority in it that we could not just dismiss it.

We spent the next day letting Lee show us what his ministry, Networks Romania, was doing through a discipleship school that ministered to the Roma (Gypsies). He would invite single young adults to the school where they would get Biblical training as they worked in the Roma community. They were mainly helping the Roma to learn how to better their lives and their community through better practices. Things like gardening, budgeting their money, and making sure their children go to school. Of course, they introduced Jesus to them through these acts of intentional kindness.

We got on a train to Croatia, and we had a lot to think about. We truly admired what Networks Romania was doing with the Roma. We had a real desire to see the work with Roma in Croatia develop further. We had already developed a relationship with two ministries in Croatia working with the Roma and have partnered with each one when bringing American/foreign teams. We worked with the Roma not only in Croatia but throughout the Balkans. As we were traveling back to Croatia and considering these things, we kept wondering how the word about serving another man's vision translated into serving our own vision. What was our vision? If we left EI, what then?

So this was January of 2015 and Zuzanna started planning the outreaches for the spring and summer. Around April, I flew down to Sofia, Bulgaria, to attend a Balkan Networks meeting and a seminar taught by George Otis Jr. George was one of my heroes because of his work with developing intercessory tools. I had read his book *Informed Intercession*, where he had laid out a strategic approach to evangelizing communities through prayer, unity, and data gathering, known as spiritual mapping. The seminar was so informative as I listened to George put into words the intercessory life I had been trying to live for many years.

There were other benefits or duties to this trip to Bulgaria. Getting to meet once again with the men and women of Balkan Networks and hearing what they were seeing God doing throughout the Balkans. Also, I had permission from Jeff to explore the possibility of future ministry with the refugee camps in Bulgaria that was set up to accommodate those fleeing the Muslim countries in the Middle East. Because of so much instability in the Middle East of radical Islamic regimes, many were fleeing to the West. I made arrangements to visit one of the camps to see what possibilities there might be. This was a humbling visit for me as I met people who had experienced and were experiencing something we in the West had never even considered. I discussed with the Bulgarian director of the camp the possibility of helping with humanitarian aid from Christian organizations. He was open to the help, but I knew there would have to be deeper negotiations. For whatever reason, further involvement with these refugees never materialized, but it had a great impact on me.

On my way back to Zagreb, I had to transfer planes in Belgrade. As we were approaching the airport in Serbia, we flew over Belgrade. Looking down on the city I began to weep. The Lord was sharing His heart with me for a city I had prayed for over so many years. Still to this day, Belgrade is at the top of my prayer list. I often feel for the people there. If I had another life to give, I would give it for Belgrade; a city that has been invaded, bombed and devastated fifty times throughout history and has always emerged from the ashes.

· · · · · ·

MORE OUTREACHES

If I remember right, there were four outreaches Zuzanna organized for EI that summer of 2015. First was a team that came from our sending church in Dallas, UPPERROOM. This team was made up of seven individuals, four ladies and three men. We ministered on the streets of Zagreb and in two Croatian Roma villages. We partnered with two different ministries in the two villages. Mainly what we did was join in by going house to house, visiting the people and then having a church service for them.

With this UPPERROOM group, we decided to go to the coast for one of their last days. We had quite an adventure on this trip. We were in two different cars—the girls in the car Zuzanna was driving, and the guys in the car I was driving. Zuzanna had the GPS and decided to take a route we had never taken before. We, in the car full of guys were following with no idea where we were. We went down dirt roads, through little villages, and up and down mountains. We kept calling them on the phone asking if they were sure of where they were leading us? We made a joke that we must be trying to find a lost-people group. Finally, we came into a clearing near the top of a mountain where we decided to stop and get out of the cars. The view was breathtaking. You could see for miles and miles all the islands and down the coast. So, we made our way down to the coast and swam in the Adriatic Sea.

Zuzanna was organizing two performances for Ballet Magnificat! in Belgrade on their 2015 European tour in the spring. This was a new adventure for us and them as this was a new country for Ballet Magnificat! Ever since that year, to the date of writing this book, Ballet Magnificat! has performed annually in Belgrade and now has added other cities within Serbia.

To help us with this event, Joe and Laura Duncan of Generations Church in Granbury, Texas, volunteered. They flew into Zagreb and then we drove to Belgrade to prepare for the event. While Laura and Zuzanna were organizing everything, Joe and I had the task of working on the set for the stage. We had to build a cage with wheels on the bottom so it was movable. This cage had to resemble a holocaust fence for the program Ballet Magnificat! would be performing—the "Hiding Place," about Corrie ten Boom during World War II. There were two performances at two different locations. One was a benefit performance for orphans and disadvantaged children and the other was at one of the main theaters in the city. For the one at the main theater, we sold tickets. I believe it was sold out; the theater was full. Zuzanna connected with two individuals in Belgrade that helped her greatly—Samuel Petrovski and a lady named Ana. They were a tremendous help with the logistics and many details.

After the Belgrade performances, we drove the Duncans down through Bosnia to Montenegro to visit the Roma refugee camp Zuzanna and I had visited the year before. The Duncans wanted to see that camp because they thought their church would want to get involved there.

First, we drove to Sarajevo to spend the night. We had some friends there who showed us the city. Sarajevo is a city where East meets West. It is famous for where World War I started and where the 1984 Winter Olympics was held. And then in the early '90s, it was a prominent battleground for the war that broke up Yugoslavia.

We drove on down from there to Podgorica, Montenegro. This was an amazing scenic drive; also treacherous. The roads were narrow and in some places real cliff-hangers. We made it to Podgorica and visited the camp the next day. If I remember right, we bought food and toys for the children. The next day we drove up the Croatian coast to Zagreb. We stopped and visited the historic city of Dubrovnik and spent the night in Makarska on our way back.

There was another outreach Zuzanna organized that summer that ministered in Budapest, Hungary, and then Serbia. I did not go on this outreach. I know they ministered to the Roma in Serbia and did street evangelism in Budapest.

The fourth group that came that summer was from Dallas. I can't remember how many were in this group, but we planned an outreach to Rijeka, Croatia. We actually stayed on a ship that had been converted into a floating hotel. It was docked in the harbor. We did some street ministry on the main walking street of the city. We mainly encountered pedestrians and witnessed to them.

Then we teamed up with Andrej Grozdanov, considered Croatia's best guitarist, for a concert-type event at a college. Some of the guys in the American team played instruments so Andrej formed them into a band to play for the students. One day we went to an area of the town where the church that was hosting us had been reaching out to the Roma. We visited some of the families but we could tell these Roma were well-off. Either way, we were a witness for the church. I think it was that same evening there was a youth meeting where two or three churches teamed up to minister to teenagers. Some of the team gave their testimonies. We then had a fun day at one of the beaches along the coast.

Back in the fall of 2014, we went to the States to fund raise. While we were there, we let it be known that we needed a car for the ministry. UPPERROOM took up an offering and provided a big chunk of the money we would need. Coupled with a few other sizable donations, we were able to purchase a 2011 Peugeot. I never dreamed of owning a French car, but I really liked that Peugeot. This helped us to be a lot more mobile than before.

Chapter Sixteen

Then June 2015 came and we had been praying about the word that had been given us earlier in the year about how we had been faithful to serve another man's vision and that it was now time that we pursue our own vision. The more Zuzanna and I prayed about it the more we felt we had to leave the organization we had been with. This was not easy, because that organization opened the door for us to return to the Balkans and to full-time ministry. We contacted our leaders and asked for a meeting. The director was coming to Zagreb with a team, so this seemed like a good time to meet in person. Since we landed in Zagreb, we set up a Balkan base for the organization. The director and the board were happy with us and the results of the past year and a half. We tried to figure out a way to implement our vision within the organization, but we were not even sure how to articulate fully our heart and vision. After a series of conversations, we submitted our resignation.

What now?

We clearly heard from the Lord that we were to start a house of prayer in Zagreb and it was to be five days a week. "OK, Lord, it is just us and we are not musicians and we are foreigners."

We knew the success our church in Dallas had by starting out as a house of prayer. We knew we did not want to start a church but just find ways to minister to others. Also, we had learned from UPPER-ROOM that we must minister to God first before we can minister to others. Then we heard the Lord say, "Take a year to minister to Me and then I will show you what to do after that."

Talking back to the Lord, "What will our supporters think if we are 'just' praying?"

He gave us peace concerning that because things started falling into place. We were about to go to the States for our usual fall visit and we would be facing our supporters. We quickly arranged for a video producer to come to Zagreb and put a video together for us promoting prayer for Zagreb. Shortly after resigning from EI, thinking about founding a new ministry, and needing a name for the ministry, a name just seemed to pop into Zuzanna's mind—Intentional Strategies for Transformation. When she first spoke that name, I immediately said, "Yes, that sounds right." Then I realized it correctly fit our vision which was to intentionally seek God's strategies for the transformation of the Balkan countries from goat nations into sheep nations, according to Matthew 25:32.

We were informed of a special prayer meeting in Timişoara, Romania. We were about to go to the States for a month and needed the time to get ready, but we just kept thinking we really needed to go to this meeting. So, we booked a hotel room and went. Two divine appointments happened while we were there.

There was a lady there who was also from Zagreb. She came up to Zuzanna and introduced herself. This was during one of the sessions, so they went out in the hall to talk. An hour-and-a-half later, the session ended—and they were still talking. Finally, Zuzanna came and found me and she had a big smile on her face. She began to tell me about this lady she had met.

Lidija lives in Zagreb, is a pastor's wife, and leads worship in her church. The most remarkable thing is that a few weeks earlier she had attended a worship workshop in Holland (I think she said it was a three-week workshop). It was conducted by the International House of Prayer in Kansas City and Youth with A Mission (YWAM). They had been taught about how prayer and worship work together. A Slovenian friend of hers had asked her to go to this European Trumpet Call in Timişoara and she came. Evidently, someone else that was to come cancelled so she asked if Lidija could come with her. Seemingly a coincidence, but God clearly arranged it.

Zuzanna and I recognized this was a divine appointment. We needed a worship leader for the house of prayer we were starting and Lidija needed a place to minister in her gift of leading worship. Although we both lived in Zagreb, God had divinely brought us together in Romania. It is so awesome when God does things like this to confirm His intentions.

So, we came to an agreement with Lidija that when we got back from the States and started back to praying five days a week that she would join us and lead the worship.

The second divine appointment and another reason God had brought us was that we met Henning Schikora. He was the director of an initiative to have extended days of prayer in all the European nations' capital cities. The way he and his group did this was to take two to three countries at a time; pray a few days in one, then travel to the next, pray there a few days and then end with prayer in the third country. He asked if we would consider organizing and hosting them in Ljubljana, Slovenia; Zagreb, Croatia; and Belgrade, Serbia. We thought this was a great initiative and we wanted to help. He did not yet have a date and time when these three countries would be on their schedule.

When we returned from the States we were still living in Zagreb in the apartment owned by the Evangelical Pentecostal Churches (EPC). We are so grateful to them for letting us rent the apartment.

We met with the director of EPC about starting a house of prayer. Although he did not understand the house of prayer concept, he was not opposed to it. There was already a church meeting on the first floor of the building and although we had not joined any church yet, we would often attend downstairs.

・・・・・・

UPPER ROOM GORNJA SOBA

We started the house of prayer in Zagreb in October 2015. Usually it was just Zuzanna, Lidija and I. Every once in a while, some others would come. Some of the members at Lidija's church would come, usually once during the week. Lidija had a son Joshua who would sometimes come and accompany her on his guitar. We had bought a piano for Lidija to use.

We were lifting up a sound of praise to the Lord over Zagreb and praying for Croatia. We needed a name for the house of prayer so we adopted Upper Room Gornja Soba Zagreb. While we were in the States we had met with the UPPERROOM Dallas pastor Michael, and he was very positive about us starting our house of prayer. Our goal at this time was to not start a church but just a place where we would invite any Christians, no matter what background or denomination, to come and pray together. This was a tremendous need as unity was in short supply among denominations in the city.

I knew the power in combining intercession and worship, so the goal at Gornja Soba was to be a launching place for us to practice the Tabernacle of David over Croatia. In my studies of the Tabernacle of David, King David had erected a tent on Mount Zion that offered up worship to God 24/7. I knew this was what Croatia needed. This was my dream to see this happen there in the capital of Zagreb. We did not feel that we were to focus on it being 24/7, but five days per week, two- hour sets. This, we felt, was a mandate from the Lord for the next season. This was still very ambitious given that we only had the three of us.

If you have never studied the Tabernacle of David (2 Samuel 6; 1 Chronicles chapters 13 thru 16), I highly encourage you to study it. You will understand the power of what King David instituted. David took the Ark of the Covenant, which to Israel was the presence of God, and put it in a tent so the public could come with free access to worship God before the Ark. This was totally contrary to the Law of Moses, where the Ark was to be behind thick curtains in the Holy of Holies of the Tabernacle and only the High Priest could visit it once a year. David had done something radical in his day, but it foreshadowed what Jesus would do through His ministry. Either way, the result was that Israel was blessed in that David was able to go out and conquer his enemies, expand the borders of Israel, plus establish a glorious kingdom for his son Solomon to rule over.

I am convinced, what we see in the actions that David took by setting up his Tabernacle is a pattern for transforming a nation into a sheep nation. David was mimicking what goes on at the Throne of God. This is what Apostle John described in his vision of the Throne of God in heaven in Revelations, Chapter Four.

To legally operate as a ministry, we needed to register as a non-government organization (NGO) in Croatia and possibly register as a 501(c)3 in America We acquired a lawyer in Zagreb who was a Christian. To the date of this writing, she is still our attorney in Zagreb and not only has she helped us establish Intentional Strategies for Transformation in Croatia, but has helped us navigate the many ins and outs of the legal system in Croatia. We chose not to register as a 501(c)3 in America.

As we met to pray, the Lord began to give us a prayer strategy for Croatia. We would take the Seven Mountains approach. The Seven Mountains is a teaching popularized by Youth with A Mission and Campus Crusade that divides up culture or society into seven spheres of influence. Those seven spheres are: Family, Religion, Government, Arts and Entertainment, Education, Media, and Business. We set up a plan of praying for two of those spheres a week in the prayer sets. Usually we would worship for the first hour and then at some point during the second hour pray for one of the spheres.

We began to see God moving in these spheres of influence. The most notable was in the business or economic mountain. There was a man who attended the prayer sets for a season in 2016 who worked as an analyst in one of the main banks of Croatia. His job was to collect data and analyze the business climate in Croatia. At one point he asked us when did we start praying for the seven spheres? We told him in the fall of 2015. He said, "That is when the economy of Croatia started turning around toward a profit margin and I have the data to prove it." This was so elevating to hear and we knew we were on the right track.

One day we were scheduled to pray for education and a lady came by divine providence to the prayer set and she asked us to pray for an educational program for children she was trying to get approved.

Then there was the day a parliamentarian from the Croatian Parliament came, and we happened to be praying for government that day. We were praying for the media one day and a lady from the state-run radio station came wanting to interview us concerning the prayer room. God was confirming what we were doing. I love it when God confirms that you are walking in His will.

Around the end of 2015, we wanted to move out of the tiny apartment on Kosirnikova so we started looking around Zagreb. We were looking for two things: A more spacious house or apartment, and also a place for the house of prayer. It would be good to find a place for us to live and have HOP also. Since we had chosen the house of prayer to be called Upper Room, a place upstairs would be fitting. We started looking around the downtown or center of Zagreb but the prices were far above our budget. Finally, we contacted an apartment-finding agency. The lady that started helping us had us looking at apartment after apartment. Almost all were either above our budget or just in odd places.

Zuzanna was also looking online, and found one that was about thirteen minutes from the city center that had lots of space and even a large room above the living area. Zuzanna really liked it but we went on to look at a few more. We decided to go back to that house on Jelenčica and look at it again. It had a nice staircase that connected the upper and lower rooms. The upper room was just perfect for a place for the Upper Room prayer room; at least twelve to fifteen people could comfortably worship there. The apartment also had three bedrooms downstairs and a large living room, plus two bathrooms and a balcony with a stunning view. The asking price was a real steal for that much space. We decided this was perfect and made plans to meet the owner. Before we met the owner, we asked Lidija to take the bus and tram from her house to the house on Jelenčica just to see how long it would take her. We didn't want it to be such a burden on her that she could no longer come lead worship. It took her over an hour, but she said she would continue even though it took so much time. We are so thankful for that sacrifice she made five days a week. So, we met with the owner and he even lowered the rent somewhat.

We moved into the house on Jelenčica around the middle of February 2016.

· · · · · ·

LIKA

That spring, the protestant leaders called for a prayer meeting in Osijek, Croatia, to pray for the country, so Zuzanna and I decided to go. It was a good gathering; most of the leaders we knew in the country were there. They had a map of the country with pins marking where there were protestant churches. Zuzanna was looking at the map and noticed there was a large area between the coast and Karlovac (close to Zagreb) that had no pins at all. She asked those standing around, "What about this blank area?" Someone said, "Oh, that is Lika; it is a big black hole. Stay away from that area." That comment really pierced Zuzanna's heart.

Well, we left the meeting and Zuzanna kept thinking about that blank area. One day a few weeks later, she said to me, "I have been thinking about that Lika area and I want to do a prayer-walk through it."

She planned out a route where she would start at the edge of the capital Zagreb and end in Šibenik (on the Adriatic coast), Croatia.

This would include some dirt roads, many abandoned villages, and bike routes, but also some main roads with much traffic.

The first day, I drove her to the city limits of Zagreb and she began to walk, praying for the homes and families along the way. I found a place along the roadside to sit and wait for her to call for me to pick her up. Then we would go back home for the night. The next day, I would drop her off at where I had picked her up the previous day. Zuzanna would walk about four to six hours covering about twenty miles. She would prayer-walk three days and then rest a day or two.

We followed this routine until we got about halfway to the coast. There was a church in the destination city of Šibenik that let us sleep in the church at night because after we got halfway, we were then closer to the coast and it was advantageous to stay there.

At first, I was skeptical about this prayer-walk. My thinking was that we needed to spend our energies on the prayer room rather than any other venture. After the second or third day of Zuzanna's walk, the Lord gave me a peace that this was Him, especially when I noticed the torture her feet were going through. While I waited for Zuzanna, I began to prayer-walk in the cities and villages of Lika. I had gotten too old to do much prayer-walking.

I remember the last day of her walk into Šibenik Zuzanna was so exhausted because she spent about seven hours that day walking over thirty miles so she could finish up.

The next day, we met with the pastor of the Šibenik church. He told us about three families that had a burden for Lika. One of them, Zuzanna had already connected with, so we decided to meet with them and the other two families also to see what could be done or just what was their vision for Lika. It amazed us that we were able to arrange a meeting with all three the same day.

Two of the families lived on the coast but one of them actually lived in Lika. We decided to meet there in Lika at that family's house one Saturday. We met and got to know each other better. We decided we would meet once a month to pray together at that family's house.

They lived in the city of Gračac, which is near the southern border of the Lika province.

We were meeting every month and having a great time of fellowship. The house had a nice big yard for the children to play. Finally, the Lord gave us a plan. We would put together a carnival-type event for the city of Gračac. We would put out a flyer in key locations around the city. We would get permission to set up in the main park of the city. Gračac has about five thousand residents. We ran into a problem with the mayor. She was skeptical of the event, mainly I think because we were a Christian group not associated with the Catholic church. She would not give us permission to use the park so we decided to hold the event in the yard where this family lived. This was in the summer of 2017.

Pin Oaks Christian Fellowship in Anna, Texas, wanted to send a team to Croatia to see our work there and to partner with us so this carnival in Gračac would be perfect. So, we finished the planning and it was successful for a first-time event on our part for Gračac. We had a bounce house for the children, clowns doing tricks, drinks and cakes for the children and adults, plus a band that had come all the way from Slavonia. Some church workers from churches on the Dalmatian coast came mainly out of curiosity to see something happening in Lika for the Lord. Not many townsfolk came, but we felt really good about the event.

The team that came from Pin Oaks was made up of five individuals: their Pastor Phil, Gary (IST's board chairman), David, Monty, and Patrice. We had another project for them: help us to start building a prayer room.

After we joined Agape Church in Zagreb, Pastor Saša offered the attic of the church for us to build out a prayer room and told us they would not charge rent as long as we invested and built it out. The attic needed a cleaning out so we thought we could get the Pin Oaks team to help us with that. We took them by the church to look at the attic. We wanted their advice also of the possibilities of building it out.

They took one look and said "No Way." They said the roof would have to be totally renewed. This was out of the question as the property belonged to the city.

Pastor Phil then asked to see the rest of the building. As we made it to the second floor, he said, "I wonder if the church would let you use this second floor?"

The team really liked that idea. We decided to talk to Pastor Saša about that possibility. Now the second floor was in a raw condition. Saša told us his plans for building out some rooms and which one we could use. The church would still give us free rent, but we would have to build a portion of the second floor out, including the room we were to use. The team from Texas then surprised us by saying they would invest the first $2000 in order to get the walls and ceiling up. This was an amazing development. So, we set out to get finished what we could before the team had to leave. They only had three days to get the materials and do what we could before they had to leave. This was just about enough time to get one wall built plus a closet.

We had been praying about moving the prayer room from our house because attendance was growing and we were starting to have problems with the neighbors concerning parking. So, the room we built out at Agape was the Lord's answer. It was near the center of the city and very convenient for people to come to.

Another thing happened in the spring of 2017. Zuzanna had been contacted by a lady who wanted to come talk to her about spiritual matters. Ana came over with her sister and we talked to them. We asked if they wanted to receive Jesus into their lives and they said yes. A few days later, Ana brought two other girls over and they asked Jesus into their lives. All together, four had asked Jesus into their lives but only two of the ladies started meeting with us in the house of prayer. They had asked Jesus into their lives before they came to us but they had rededicated their lives in our living room. Ana and Ksenjia continued to come and while the team from Pin Oaks was there, we baptized them. I remember especially that when Ksenjia she came back up out of the water, I had a word for her that God had something special for her.

The day the Pin Oaks team left, Zuzanna also left for the States. We saved money by my not going with her on this trip. The next Sunday, she met with the UPPERROOM pastor, Michael, before the service and he inquired about Zagreb. She told him we had acquired a new place for the Upper Room Zagreb and she needed to raise money for the final build-out and sound equipment. Michael said that he would call her up and she could give testimony of what was happening and then he would ask people to give. We were amazed when over $8,000 was given. She immediately emailed me that God was doing a quick work concerning the prayer room in Zagreb. So, I told Pastor Saša to arrange for the workers to finish out the prayer room.

Lidija had been on vacation for two weeks, and when she returned I told her about the fact we would be moving soon and she seemed surprised. Zuzanna and I had already noticed Lidija was having a hard time balancing her time between her commitment to the prayer room, her duties as a pastor's wife, and her involvement with a women's mission group in the Balkans. One evening after the prayer set, she and I talked about her future with the prayer room. I let her know we had noticed her extensive involvement in many things and we would not be surprised if she was about to leave us. We decided that when Zuzanna got back from America we would talk it over. In the end, Lidija left us to go on to further her calling, but we all felt great peace about this as Zuzanna and I also felt that it was a new chapter in the life of Upper Room Zagreb

So, the Upper Room Zagreb was finished out in about a month. We had enough money to buy the needed quality music and sound equipment. I think it was September 2017 we were in a well-equipped upper room near the center of the city with plenty of parking. Every time we met, five times a week, we never knew how many people would come. Many times it was just Zuzanna and I and on other days many would come. After Lidija left, we had no worship leader so we would tune into YouTube recordings of the prayer sets at UPPER-ROOM Dallas. We were amazed at how much these recordings ministered to us. The Lord always showed up and manifested in the room in some special way. Many people would come for a while but then stop coming. Everyone said God was doing something special in their lives. Maybe they just needed a season with the Lord.

A few people kept coming back. Like Andrea, who ended up becoming a prayer leader. Then there was Zora, an older lady but very young in spirit who came once or twice a week. Sara started coming and later her husband Marko came also. And there was Iva who had started coming when we were still in our house. Iva would get so blasted by the Holy Spirit that sometimes she would stay at least an hour or more after the set, unable to move. When we moved to the new place, Iva started leading prayer sets also.

Then Ksenija started coming back regularly and also her cousin Ana—the two who had prayed with us in our living room.

Chapter Seventeen

We had taken a year to pray and seek the Lord. We are so thankful to our supporters for that year as they continued to believe in us and our mission. By the beginning of 2017, we knew the Lord's direction for Intentional Strategies for Transformation: the prayer room in Zagreb, the work in Lika. And we wanted to continue investing into the Ceuas village in Romania.

As for the prayer room, we continued to be open to all churches in the city. We were aware that God was using us for unity of His body, the Church with a big C. We were fervent in praying for unity and against the religious spirit that divided many churches from working together. We were careful not to take sides in any possible differences or conflicts, but were there to pray for the spirit of unity to flood the nation. We were continuing to pray for the seven mountains of Croatia.

In Lika, we continued the once-a-month prayer gatherings with families. One of the families stopped coming because they really had their hearts set on another part of Lika. Before the year was over, the Zuban family bought land with a house on it in a village just outside Gračac. The house had been all but destroyed during the war. A Serb family had to leave it behind when the war came in 1991 or '92. Vandals had come in and gutted the house from anything valuable, like doors, windows and pipes.

Centuries of history in Lika repeated itself once again when it was in the city of Knin, just south east of Gračac that the war that broke up Yugoslavia had begun. No war is easy, but this war was devastating to the region and the people it impacted on all sides. In the end, the Serbs were not able to hold the land and had to flee.

Vanko Zuban, the father of the family that was buying the house, had to make a trip to Serbia to meet with the owner in order to make the purchase and get the papers of transfer signed. Vanko said it was a very emotional meeting with the owner because he was having to sell the home that he had spent a better part of his life building. Vanko said he cried with the man as he signed the land over. The Serb owner in the end was glad that a good man, though Croatian, was buying his family's house.

As you study the history of Lika, it will break your heart. It has been the ground where empires met in battle over the centuries. Civilizations have risen and fallen, century after century.

· · · · · ·

BUCKNER IN ROMANIA

When we left European Initiative, we still stayed connected with Buckner in Romania. Our contact in Targu Mures, Daci, is the director of Buckner Romania. Buckner Romania was originally started by Buckner Orphans Home in Dallas, Texas. There was a point back a few years ago when I understand Buckner Dallas could not support the work in Romania anymore so Buckner Romania had to become independent.

Daci had the wisdom to carry the burden and maintain their amazing work with gypsy children. Their program is quite unique. They have the gypsy children come to them early in the morning where they feed them an early breakfast, have the children change into clean clothes, and then Buckner transports them to school. After school, Buckner picks up the children, brings them to the center, helps them with their homework, feeds them a hearty meal, changes them back into the clothes they wore that morning, and sends them home to their family. Also, they help the older teenagers learn a skill through different programs they offer. I hold up Daci in high honor for what he has managed to create for the underprivileged in Targu Mures, Romania.

Daci took us to a village called Caues. We could not believe the poverty we saw. There were families almost living like animals. We had brought clothes and food to give to the families, but we wanted to do something that would have a long-lasting effect. Daci and Zuzanna came up with a plan. We were going to start an after-school tutoring program. The situation was that the gypsy children from this village would attend a nearby school, but the teachers did not speak the children's language. So, what was happening was the teachers would ignore these children and they never learned anything. The plan was that we would choose twelve children that showed promise and set up the program for them. The teacher would be there when the children got out of their regular classes; the teacher/tutor would feed them lunch and then basically re-teach everything they were supposed to learn that morning, but in their language. Also, she would begin to teach them Romanian, so that they could assimilate into society. We started with a group of first graders and wanted to carry them through as many years as we could. It was remarkable to watch these children learn how to read and write; some of the first ones in the village to do so.

We at IST adopted that program and ran it for three years. Before the fourth year, God spoke to Zuzanna with great clarity that it was time to turn over this program to Buckner Romania. We knew that we had done what God wanted us to do and now we needed to let go and concentrate on Croatia. It broke our hearts to give up that ministry for those children, but we know that we had made a difference in these special and very needy children who learned to read and write where they would not have had that opportunity before.

The year 2017 ended with us in a new location for the prayer room in Zagreb and having our presence more visible in Gračac.

New Year's Day 2018, I found myself boarding a plane for America. My brother-in-law, Stuart Gurley, was in fourth stage stomach cancer and my sister needed help. I got back to Dallas and started helping with things that needed to be done. By this time, Stuart had a hospital bed plus hospice care. So, there was not much for me to do but pray and provide emotional support for Glenda. It was hard to see this once strong man having to go through these horrible days. On January 12, Stuart passed on to heaven. Just to think of how much he is now enjoying heaven after suffering many troubles in this life helped me to see God's wisdom of the cycle of life we must endure on this earth. After the troubles of this life, we will appreciate heaven so much that rebellion against God will be unthinkable.

Before returning to Croatia, I flew to Nevada to visit Gordon and his family. Dakota was about five months old and Cheyenne was almost three. I spent three days with them. The first day I pulled up some videos on YouTube of Donald Duck for Cheyenne. All the time I was there she wanted to watch Donald Duck.

From Nevada, I flew to Salt Lake City where Asa picked me up and I spent a couple of days with him. This was the first time I had been to where Asa had been living for the past few years. I met some nice people there. Of course, Asa never has trouble making friends, but these people are really special. They have a home church and I ministered one evening in their meeting.

I flew back to Dallas and spent a few days with Joy before flying back to Croatia on February 12. It was so good to get back to the Zagreb prayer room. I had missed the worship and devotional time. Shortly after returning we were hosting the Balkan Network meeting in Croatia. Those that came: Philip and Rosey from Bulgaria, Barry from Albania, Kati from Albania, The Bailer family from Albania, Bryan from Macedonia, Venco and Kata from Macedonia, Lee and James from Romania, Robert from Bosnia, plus Zuzanna and I. So Albania, Bosnia, Bulgaria, Croatia, Macedonia and Romania were all represented. The participants came on the 15th and left on the 18th.

We had a great time encouraging each other and sharing about the ministries we were involved in. It was always enriching to go to the annual Balkan Networks meetings and see what God was doing all across the Balkans.

······

LIFE AND MINISTRY IN THE BALKANS

Shortly after the Balkan Networks meeting, the UPPERROOM team from Denver came. The team was made up of Joanna, Sean and Jennifer Fitzgerald, Kristen, Donny and Mia. They came to minister to Zuzanna and me, plus the teams we worked with in Croatia. The first thing they did was take over our kitchen and would not let us do any cooking. Donny and Mia even came a day earlier and bought food. Mia, being a nutritionist, planned the meals and did most of the cooking. I will always remember the sacrifice they made to come minister to us and to our team. They spoke wisdom into our lives and prepared us for ministry ahead. This was a pastoral visit we absolutely needed. They left on Saturday Feb. 24th.

Remember Henning, the man we had met in Romania in 2015 at the European Trumpet Call? He asked Zuzanna if she would organize the Operation Capitals of Europe (OCE) prayer initiative in Slovenia, Croatia and Serbia. This prayer initiative was so powerful. We started by praying in Slovenia. Strategic places in and around the capital, Ljubljana, were selected to pray over. We especially noticed the evil-looking statues and artwork displayed around the city. We divided into two teams. The team I was in went to the source of the Sava River where we prayed. We did a prophetic act by pouring wine and salt into the river. The Sava River flows through all three countries we were praying for.

We then went to Zagreb to pray for Croatia. We selected two key places to pray—the castle that overlooks the city, and the key intersection of Vukovara Road and Hrvatske Bratske Zajednice Road. The team that was from OCE was actually a discipleship training school and this was part of their curriculum. While in Zagreb, the team had to attend several days of lectures on the Motivational Gifts listed in Romans 12. We got to sit in on this and that was a real treat. If you have never done an in-depth study of the motivational gifts, I suggest you do so. It will really help you discover why God made you the way you are and show you why you are motivated to act the way you do. Sometimes they are called redemptive gifts.

Then we went to pray in Belgrade, Serbia. We prayed at the government buildings, at the Danube River, and more. I especially was moved when we prayed at the end of the Sava River where it pours into the Danube.

In 2017, a family in Tulsa, Oklahoma, made contact with us as they were interested in coming to Croatia as missionaries. During our fall fundraising trip, we went to Tulsa to meet with them. We spent a few days with them so we could get to know each other, and having met their church leadership, parents and friends, we decided to help them come to Croatia and work with us.

Finally, when all the paperwork had been completed, the Thomsons flew into Croatia in the spring of 2018. They were to stay with us until they found their own place. Within a month they had not only found a place to live but had purchased a car. Through our NGO, IST, we covered them with a residency visa until they found their place working with a local church, which would provide a visa for them.

Shortly after the Thomsons came, Genna Sidler arrived to stay a week with us. Thank the Lord for the large apartment He provided for us so we could host multiple people at the same time. Genna did a professional video shoot of the IST ministry, which we needed for presentations.

On March 10th, Genna, Zuzanna and I went to Gračac. It was an amazing time. Friday, Vanko and Blanka signed the papers to buy their house in Gračac. This was another step forward into Lika.

Genna and Zuzanna then went on to Romania where Genna also shot some video footage of the work with the after-school program in the Caues village.

The last week of March 2018, Zuzanna and I went to Subotica, Serbia. Hajnalka (Zuzanna's sister), Babuci (her niece), and Zuzanna wanted to go visit their brothers and their families in Vienna, Austria. Viktor, my pastor friend in Subotica, had asked me a few months earlier if I could come spend a few days with him. So, I thought this would be a good time to do that. Zuzanna dropped me off at Viktor and Ksenija's on their way out of town.

It was always great to be in their home. Ksenija is one of the best cooks I know. It is always a delight to sit down at her table. My plans with Viktor were to just shadow him as he did ministry. Friday evening, we had a time with his workers in his church. I gave a greeting and spoke some things into their lives. Then on Saturday morning, we went to Pivnica, Serbia, for a meeting of the network of churches Viktor oversaw. That was an amazing time. This group of seventeen pastors and workers showed such unity, which is an uncommon thing in the Balkans. There were Serbs, Roma and Hungarian pastors all working together. The fellowship was wonderful. There was such love for one another. I shared some encouraging words in the meeting. At one point, I disrupted the meeting because the chair I was sitting on just collapsed. I wasn't hurt so everyone laughed and they got me another chair.

Back in 2017, the Intentional Strategies for Transformation (IST) group had been invited to participate with an organization called Lausanne. I was familiar with the Lausanne group because I remember it being formed some forty years ago in Lausanne, Switzerland by the Billy Graham organization and other big-name evangelical groups. Their goal was to come in unity to do evangelism across the globe. Since IST was very tuned in to the need for unity in Croatia, we were glad to be involved. At the meetings, they would often ask us to present our ministry. We always invited them to the prayer room, which we always regarded as a place for all Christians to come together and pray together.

By April 2018, we were attending the third or fourth meeting of the Lausanne group. Zuzanna had been elected to the core board. They were working on an event for Christmas that all the member churches could participate in for an outreach in the capital of Zagreb. The plans were to use the annual Advent celebrations in Zagreb that were sponsored by the city to promote Christmas events. The city always erected a large stage in the main square of the city and then they would invite groups, NGOs, churches, etc. to use the stage for presentations that related to Christmas. The stage would be up all of December until New Year's. Some of the churches had taken advantage of this for years to showcase their ministry, choirs or bands. Lausanne group used the stage one evening and many of the churches combined their people and formed a mega choir, plus performed some skits and had a unique band. Then the following night they rented an auditorium where they had an evangelical outreach. The hall was full with about 300 to 350 people.

· · · · · ·

OUR NEW FRIENDS— THE CHARISMATIC CATHOLICS

In either March or April 2017, I decided to go to a conference in Slavonski Brod, Croatia, called Vatra (Fire). This was an annual conference that the Charismatic Catholics did each year. We had been hearing about a house of prayer in Slavonski Brod run by the Charismatic Catholics so I decided to go. I was totally blown away by the worship. There must have been two hundred people doing worship and listening to speakers. These Catholics were worshiping Jesus with all their hearts. If I hadn't known ahead of time, I would have thought they were just ordinary Charismatics. The conference was organized by the Slavonski Brod House of Prayer. The Slavonski Brod HOP is a section of a house where the Pešorda family lived. The father and mother are Bartol and Biljana, and they have eight children. Most all of them play instruments. Their house is up on a hill that overlooks the city and you can actually see over into Bosnia. From their house you can also see the highway that leads east toward Serbia.

Later that year, Zuzanna and I decided we needed to go visit them. We were welcomed with open arms. After an afternoon of visiting, mainly with Bartol and Biljana, we were amazed at how much we had in common. They told us of how they were in an odd situation as Charismatic Catholics. The Catholic hierarchy treated them like they were Protestants and the Protestants couldn't understand why they would not leave the Catholic Church. They were being criticized by both sides. Meeting these Charismatic Catholics and seeing their love for Jesus was more convincing evidence to me that no matter what label a church puts on the building, there are members that have had a real encounter with Jesus.

······

STREET MINISTRY

While we lived in the Balkans, I loved to go witnessing on the streets. Normally I am shy and introverted. I do believe God helped me overcome that back in my days of teaching. I still struggle at times with shyness, but I know now God wants me to break out of that and be bold. Also, back when we first started going to UPPERROOM in Dallas, I began to really enjoy stepping out for the Lord. I had been witnessing to people most of my Christian life but before, I usually came around to it in an odd way. In the past, I had to push myself to witness to strangers but now I had found a freedom of just letting Jesus flow out of me naturally.

In Croatia, I found a formula that worked great. I called it the intimate, compassion, expectation formula. I would spend time with the Lord in prayer and worship. Then I would ask Jesus for His compassion for others. Next, I would expect Him to put expectation in my heart/mind. I would then go out into the city, usually on the buses and trams or I would go to the main square. Sometimes I would ask the Lord where to go and sometimes I would just go. I would then let the Lord spotlight someone to me to approach. I would then approach them "with His compassion." Usually, I would start the conversation with, "Do you speak English?" I found out quickly that if the person was forty years old or younger, they tended to speak English. Then I would say something like, "What a beautiful country you have." They would agree and would ask me, "Are you a tourist?" Then I would reply, "Actually, I'm not. I live here." Then I would notice their astonishment as they often would reply with, "Why would you want to live here?"

This is when I would really check with the Holy Spirit about how to answer. Sometimes I would say, "I am retired, so Croatia is a great place to live." Or I might say, "I am retired and my wife works here and I help her." Maybe this would lead to talking about working with churches in a humanitarian way or the fact that we run an NGO. I would just let the Holy Spirit guide.

Often, I would come to the point where I would say, "Let me tell you the real reason I came here to Croatia." Then I knew I really had their attention. "God told me to come here and pray for your nation." Almost always I would get a puzzled look. Then I would begin to tell them about how much God loves Croatia and the people of Croatia. How He had created such a beautiful country for them to live in.

Then I would zero in on how much God loved them personally. Then the Holy Spirit would either soften their hearts or up would jump the enemy to disrupt things. Rarely did I get to lead them to salvation, but I sure planted questions in their minds.

I tried to always carry some Croatian New Testaments with me, and I would insist they take it as a gift from me. I would stress to them just how much wisdom Jesus had to share and it was all right there in the New Testament.

If they really spoke or read English well, I would give them a copy of Mike Moore's book, *Love God, Hate Church*. I know that is a controversial title, but it really is a simple approach to the Gospel for those that have turned away from the traditional churches. Most Croatians have a negative view of the churches because of the ritual approach. After Mike Moore wrote his book, I had to read it because of the title. Then when I assessed the religious climate of Croatians, I realized how this book fit their needs and mindset. I told Mike about it and he made a donation to our ministry of eighty copies.

2018 was a special year. We had a team of mainly young people come from UPPERROOM Dallas. There were fourteen in all in the group. It was led by Aaron and Sara Beth Smith (at that time the youth pastor at UPPERROOM Dallas), and also Traes Howard, his wife Donna, and their three children. All together, they were with us for ten days, June 11–21. They flew in on a Monday and spent the night in our apartment. Really crowded but we made it work.

The next morning, we went to Slavonski Brod and had a wonderful afternoon with our Charismatic Catholic friends there. The UPPERROOM Dallas team then led worship in the Slavonski Brod HOP that evening. These were some powerful times of prayer. We spent the night there and the next morning—Wednesday, June 13—we crossed the border into Bosnia and traveled to Sarajevo. We did some touring of the city in the afternoon and that evening the UR team once again led worship in the Sarajevo House of Prayer.

Then the next morning, June 14, we left Sarajevo early and made our way across Bosnia toward the Plitvica Lakes in Croatia. We were praying it would not be raining at the lakes but when we got there there was a heavy mist. The team seemed to enjoy the waterfalls at the lakes but some of them were not dressed for a rainy cool day.

We then traveled on to Primošten to spend the night. Vanko and Blanka, our good friends and coworkers in Lika, have a coastal house they rent out and that is where we were staying.

The next day was a day on the beach there in Primošten. Everyone had a great time.

Then on Saturday, we drove to Zadar and toured the seafront. Zadar is one of the oldest towns along the coast and some believe that the Apostle Paul could have preached there in his day. Then there is the Sea Organ, a unique tourist attraction along the seashore. They have built a dock that has holes crafted in such a way that the waves cause sounds like an organ.

That Saturday afternoon the UR team ministered in a church in Šibenik and Traes preached. After the service we traveled all the way back to Zagreb.

The next morning, Sunday the 17th, the team ministered in the Agape Church, our home church. The team provided worship and Aaron preached. The evening was spent at the Thomsons' house where we had a cookout. Some Hungarian young adults that had come to church that morning especially to see the team minister had been following UR Dallas on YouTube. They joined us at the cookout.

Then Monday came. We started four days of worship every evening. This was an Upper Room Zagreb event and many new guests came. Everyone was so blessed. On the last day, the team went to a Roma village to hang out and minister. This was amazing for them to see how the Roma live. Friday morning, bright and early, they flew out, back to the United States.

The Zagreb house of prayer continued to grow and mature. How satisfying to see Croatians starting to step up to lead the prayer sets. We were beginning to see our heart's desire become a reality, as the prayer room was slowly becoming more and more culturally Croatian.

We went back to America in July for several reasons. Of course we wanted to spend some time with our children, but our friend

Michelle also offered to host a fundraising banquet. This was to be our first one ever. She did such an amazing job that we will forever be so thankful as we know this was a great sacrifice for her and her family. It never ceases to amaze us how God would always bring the right people along to help us just at the right time.

Saša, our Croatian pastor, flew into Dallas too and stayed a few days with us. He went to UPPERRROOM Dallas with us on Sunday morning and after church we met with Pastor Michael and Lorisa. It was great to have the Millers meet a Croatian pastor, and we were really glad that Saša got to experience UPPERROOM.

The travels continued. Saša, Zuzanna and I went to Alabama as the guests of Barry and Robin. We attended the Grow conference at the Church of the Highlands. This was an annual conference for pastors and church leaders, and Barry thought that it could be of benefit to pastors from the Balkans. Victor also flew in from Serbia. We were there for five days. The sheer size of the place and the huge number of attendees at the conference were hard for these pastors to see in a Balkan context.

After Alabama, Zuzanna and I went back to Texas for another week or so and then we went to Las Vegas to see Gordon, Lauren and the girls. Joy went with us. Loved being there; it was fun to be around the girls. On August 18, we flew back to Croatia.

· · · · · ·

LOVE ONE ANOTHER

We had to get back in the groove fast as August 24th we had eight guests from UPPERROOM Denver arrive. They came to teach a worship workshop sponsored by IST in Zagreb. We had over a hundred people express their interest. To our surprise, many Charismatic Catholics have shown high interest. At the time of this writing, there is still a pretty deep separation between Protestants and Catholics in

Croatia. Wounds go back many centuries as there have been many unjust persecutions on the part of both parties.

We had good relations with the evangelical churches in Croatia, and we were building relationships with Charismatic Catholics. Most evangelicals did not understand the Charismatic Catholics. For that matter, we did not fully understand them either. All we knew was that God was moving in their midst and we could not stand in the way.

At IST, one of the mandates the Lord gave us was to champion unity in the body of Christ. That had to include Charismatic Catholics and regular Catholics, both who have accepted Jesus as their savior, and also those Christians who disliked Catholics. We prayed a lot that the Lord would help us to walk this fine line. Sometime that summer after we had met the Charismatic Catholics at the worship nights, we invited them over to our house. I think about fifteen came over. The more we talked, the more we knew that the same Spirit operated in us. They were also listening to the same preachers in the states on video that we were.

Zuzanna and I had asked them to give their testimonies. One by one they spoke of their encounters with Jesus. We were amazed; they all gave Jesus the glory as they told how they invited Him to come into their lives. Truly these Charismatic Catholics had been born again.

The team from Denver really blessed the people in Zagreb. The biggest thing that was communicated by the team was their love for one another. Several Croatians noticed this and mentioned it to us. On the team were Sean and Jenny and their two girls, Taylor and Michaella, and Kristin, Beth, and Kelly.

There is something else I need to plug in here. The worship workshop was attended by some local Charismatic Catholics. Actually, the previous year, when the UPPERROOM Dallas team came, one of the Catholic ladies told us of their divine appointment that drew them to come. We had publicized the event on Facebook. This lady was talking to a friend of hers about how she had listened to a new worship group/church on YouTube and they were really good. She had said to herself, "It would be amazing to hear them live."

Her friend asked, "What was the name of the group?"

She replied, "UPPERROOM".

Then her friend said, "I just saw on Facebook that they will be here in Zagreb."

This was a divine appointment because among this group were the leaders of the most popular Christian band in Croatia. That is how we initially became friends with the Charismatic Catholics in Zagreb.

The day they left, a young lady we deeply love arrived from Poland. Barbara is Polish and two years prior she was an exchange student in Zagreb. She and I connected at an event and she started coming to the prayer room. She went through a dramatic character change just in the presence of Jesus. She now lived in Krakow, Poland, and she took a vacation from work and came to stay with us for ten days. She was so helpful around the house, just serving.

Thursday, October 11th we went to Sarajevo for a twenty-four-hour burn event, held by the HOP in Sarajevo. Ten nations were represented. Gerson and his wife, Heike, have a room under their garage where they have prayer sets. There was a Burn Wagon team that came and led the event. All were Europeans from many countries. At the event, which went from twelve noon Friday to twelve noon Saturday, Zuzanna and I led a two-hour session, and we prayed for the Balkan countries according to the Seven Mountains of influence. These twenty-four hours and all-night prayer times are so good for the Balkan countries. I love to be around intercessors.

On the way to Bosnia, we stopped and picked up Bartol in Slavonski Brod. I spent the whole time while driving to Sarajevo telling him my testimony. God was making us close friends. (Zuzanna translated)

We set up a time to meet with Peter and Ana Buljan for coffee at a café near their home. They are the leaders of that worship band I mentioned before, called Božja pobjeda (God's victory). Our hearts were so in tune that after four hours we had to force ourselves to leave.

You know how it is when you meet a new believer, and your spirits just link up in the joy of the Lord. They were full of the Holy Spirit.

In October Yonathan and Miru, the Argentine young evangelist, and his wife came to minister in Zagreb. Yonathan preached three messages at Agape church Friday evening and two Saturday as a seminar. Then he preached Sunday morning at the regular Sunday service. We always loved having Yonathan come. He carries such a revival spirit about him and it is contagious!

Early Monday morning, Zuzanna flew out to the Netherlands for a "Europe Shall Be Saved" planning meeting. She had a great time in the Netherlands with Christian movers and shakers of Europe. She returned really energized about all God is doing in Europe. She met some influential people and listened to their plans to continue Awakening Europe, which is a partner organization to Europe Shall Be Saved. These Awakening Europe stadium events draw 20,000 to 30,000.

We went to a Charismatic Catholic Worship concert packed with about two thousand. It was totally led by the Charismatic Catholic worship band Bozja Pobjeta/God's Victory. And to think the leaders of this group were in our living room about a month ago. It was awesome to see what God is doing among the Charismatic Catholics. These guys would be seeking us out, just wanting to spend time with us. We did the same thing, as we had kindred spirits. We both had such a high value for worship.

One day we went to the Charismatic Catholics' regular meeting and were amazed that at least two hundred young adults were jammed into a small Catholic cathedral with another hundred outside. They were worshiping the Lord in spirit and truth; modern worship that was spontaneous at times. Although there was some liturgy in the meeting, it was all biblical. While we were attending this meeting, I remembered a prayer of mine. Having entered many Catholic and Orthodox churches over the years, mainly just looking around, I have prayed that these magnificent cathedrals would be filled with people worshiping Jesus, clapping and having hands raised. Well now I can say I have seen it. From what I am seeing, there is a healthy move of God among the Croatian Catholics.

Meanwhile, with our Lika and prayer-room teams, we were having them study the motivational gifts in Romans 12: 4-8. For as we have many members in one body, but all the members do not have the same function, so we, being many, are one body in Christ, and individually members of one another. Having then gifts differing according to the grace that is given to us, let us use them: if prophecy, let us prophesy in proportion to our faith; or ministry, let us use it in our ministering; he who teaches, in teaching; he who exhorts, in exhortation; he who gives, with liberality; he who leads, with diligence; he who shows mercy, with cheerfulness.

This helped us to discover our giftings and to respect why we view things the way we do. God has designed us individually to be strong in one or more of these gifts. They are called motivational gifts because we seem to view things and react according to the gift where we are strongest. I remember going to a motivational gift seminar as a young Christian and it gave me such revelation on how to relate to others in the body of Christ. It also helped me to understand why I act and approach ministry the way I do. I encourage all Christians to go through a motivational gift study. *My* strong gift is Mercy.

• • • • • •

A WORD OF ENCOURAGEMENT

In November, Cliff Luckhurst, a dear brother in Croatia, who is English and has been a missionary in the Balkans for many years, sent Zuzanna and me a message. He said the Lord woke him up at 3:15 a.m. and gave him a message for us. Cliff was highly respected in Croatia, so this message carried weight.

Message: *Dear Friends,*
I woke up at 3:15 a.m. with a word from the Lord for you.
"You are to stretch out (I saw hands stretched out) to have a wider area of influence.
You are to stand on tiptoe(s) to see deeper into Heaven's purposes.
For I, the Lord, will give you a wider and deeper influence in Heaven and on earth."
God bless you.
Love Cliff

This message felt good. It seemed that the Lord has found us worthy of greater responsibility. It came at a key time when we could use some encouragement.

The first weekend in December was amazing and historic in a way. IST group partnered with fifteen churches in Zagreb to organize three events to bless the city. First was a children's event and we used a Super Book video to communicate to about two hundred fifty children the love of Jesus. Most of these children were from non-Christian homes.

Later that evening, there was the main event where we filled an auditorium with over six hundred people. Most of these people were from churches but they were encouraged to bring lost friends. The new pastor from the Baptist church in the center, Ivica Horvat, preached. At the end, he prayed a prayer of salvation and encouraged those who prayed to talk to their friend who brought them.

Then the third event was held on the main square. Every year the city sets up a stage and invites local churches, NGOs and other organizations to participate in the Advent Season with Christmas presentations. So, we had a Jazz band and choir that sang Christmas songs. There was a large audience. Also, the church we go to did a mime skit about someone losing their way in worldly vices and being rescued by Jesus.

The main thing about these events was that the Gospel was presented in open forums. The underlying impact was that fifteen churches, fifteen pastors united together to work with each other. We are seeing big changes as pastors put aside their own agenda to work together for the sake of unity. This is a testimony to me that underscores the unity Jesus talked about. In unity, you can do big events that get attention in the culture. There are two main elements to seeing revival in a city/country: prayer and unity among believers. We have been praying in the house of prayer for this unity to happen and God is answering those prayers.

It is amazing how prevailing prayer works. We pray with expectation and God answers. He doesn't always answer like we expect but He will orchestrate something that shows His glory and wisdom. He always answers in His time. He is so glad we come to Him with the concerns at hand asking for His intervention. Often, we are tested to the point of "hope deferred," as we wait for the answer. Once the Lord told me that He waits for us to be burdened by an injustice, so we then cry out to Him. Then He starts working on the situation. Many factors have to be changed in order for the concern to actually change. God first of all is happy that we see the need for His involvement. He wants us to partner with Him so He can use the concern to develop our walk with Him. As we wait on Him, our dependence and confidence in Him grows. He is able to get us ready for the change. Also, all the people that will be affected by the answer to our prayer have to be ready also. Rarely do you see instant change. There must be a convergence of all God's plans for the real change to come and have a lasting effect. The result God brings will amaze us of His love and wisdom.

Zuzanna and I were alone on Christmas Day. We miss our kids and family. Holidays can be really lonely. Many Croatian Evangelical Christians do not celebrate Christmas due to their differences with the Catholic Church. We respect their feelings but we will gladly celebrate Jesus any day.

On the 28th of December we had our first IST staff Christmas party. Zuzanna really put a lot into it to make it special. We even bought a new table so we could seat everyone. We bought something special for every family. Roni and Sandra and their children came. Vanko and Blanka and their children. Nick and Danielle and their children. Marko and Sara, Igor, and Eva.

It is always a highlight when our children get to come and visit. Asa and Joy have visited several times, but Gordon and his family have never made the trip. It is, of course, not so easy with little children. It was so good to have Joy come and spend New Year's and most of January with us. We traveled to the coast, to Krka National Park, and then on to Plitvice Lakes National Park. Plitvice is a series of seven lakes that have waterfalls that flow down through the mountains, each lake pouring into the next. It is a must-see place to go if you visit Croatia.

Right after Joy left, we were contacted by a former pastor named Jon Dunn, and a former elder, Norm Fredricks, from Shady Grove Church, that they were going to be in Zagreb and wanted to meet with us. This was such a highlight for us so see them and especially to see them in Zagreb. They ministered to us and our community with advice and encouragement.

Connections just kept happening. Zuzanna spoke with a man who had become quite vocal for the Lord in the Croatian Parliament. She told him about the house of prayer and how we pray for the government. He said he wanted to come to our home and he did. He is quite an interesting guy. Talks a lot. We prayed over him and talked for an hour afterward. It is fascinating to see how God orchestrates our ministry and gives little bitty Upperroom Zagreb such influence sometimes. It is puzzling to us even now.

In February of 2019, we had a pastoral team visit us from UPPERROOM Dallas and Denver. Treas Howard, Pastor Kevin, from Dallas; Joanna, our newly elected IST board member from Denver, and also Beth and Kelly from Denver.

This visit was different from previous visits in that it was much more pastoral. The team debriefed us and our past five years in the field. They ministered to some very real-felt needs and it was so very encouraging to hear their hearts toward us and the work in Croatia. God was deepening our unity with UPPERROOM, with each visit or team they sent us.

One of the nights during their visit, we invited some Charismatic Catholics over to our house so that the UPPERROOM team could meet them. We really had a good time in fellowship. There was a time of worship and then the spirit of prophecy fell on the room. Before the night was over, everyone was prophesied over. God really showed up in our living room.

On Tuesday, Zuzanna, Marko and Sara led the prayer set. The UPPERROOM team was to observe and to evaluate. Overall, they had a good report to give. I personally felt they did really well, but I don't know that much about the dynamics of a good prayer set.

Personally, I like to back up the set with scripture. The Lord usually helps me find the right scriptures to lead. I realize He is in control. I try not to worry about other people's experience, although I am praying for Jesus to touch them. I thank the Lord that He has taught me to yield to the Spirit quickly. When I am not leading, I try to have a personal encounter with the Lord. It is almost like I press in on my own no matter how the set is being led. I do stay conscious of where the set is going in case the Spirit wants me to contribute.

The Saturday evening before the team left, Traes and Marko did a worship night in the Agape meeting room below the Upperroom Gornja soba. This was an amazing night and many of the Catholics came. Also, there was a lady there from the radio station in Zagreb. She was a reporter for religion, and she asked if she could set up an interview with us. She and Zuzanna set up an interview for the following Tuesday. So often God would open doors for us that we never sought to go through.

Each spring, the Charismatic Catholic House of Prayer in Slavonski Brod organizes a gathering called Vatra (Fire). At this Vatra in 2019, Bartol, the leader of the event, asked me to share for about thirty minutes. About six hundred were expected to attend. Now, in European terms, this is considered to be a very big thing and especially for Croatia. This House of Prayer spends much quality time praying and preparing for this event each year, and this year was no exception.

As we arrived at the venue we could feel the hunger in the place. God was there. As I shared my story, I focused on destiny. Many were moved and some came and talked with me afterwards. Prayer stations had been set up so that people could come each day to ask for prayer for their personal needs. We were so moved by the open hearts; by their simple faith that God will answer. Each time, so many would stand in line that we could not finish before the next session would start. At Zuzanna's and my station, words of knowledge, wisdom and prophesy were flowing like a river for those seeking prayer. God so honors simple faith, and desperate hearts.

Now you might think this to be fairly normal, but in the Balkans we do not see this kind of hunger and openness often. There are cultural barriers that tend to keep people closed to the real problems they are dealing with and distrust can be a strong and tall wall to overcome.

In the years we have lived in our apartment on Jelenčica, we have had many ministers traveling through or coming to minister in Croatia. Most months we will have one to three separate teams or individuals come to stay with us. I like to say that in our home "Kingdom people" are coming and going. One example: Randy and Callie, founders of Prepare International, come from Texas and minister in many countries around the world; Callie and four of her coworkers have been coming to Croatia for many years ministering to many of the churches here. We went out into the city and prayed in key places. We also drove them to Lika and prayed over the city of Gračac. These times are so important as they all contribute to the coming outpouring of God's glory on the Balkans.

The medical system in this part of the world leaves much to be desired. I had an eye exam coming up to check for glaucoma and cataracts. I went to my general practitioner back in October 2018, because I had to get a referral for this kind of an eye exam. The next available appointment was May, 30, 2019. Socialized medicine is so backwards.

······

SISAK

Last Wednesday, I went to Sisak, a city about thirty-five miles south of Zagreb. For the past year, I have had the city on my mind. I realized it had to be a spiritual thing. All I knew about this city was that there was a man that once was a pastor in a church there, but he and his family were asked to leave. I don't know why they had to leave, but that information caused me to have a burden for that city. God does this with me a lot. I will hear something and I develop a burden to pray. I pray until that burden lifts and many times I never find out what, if anything, has happened, but I know that I obeyed God's directive for me to pray. That is my part and that is good enough for me.

Anyway, I went to Sisak to do a prayer-walk. I did some research on the city and found some interesting things. There, in Sisak, is where three rivers merge. At least two of the rivers, Kupa and Odra, flow into the Sava River that flows on down to Belgrade and into the Danube. Also, and this is very important, Sisak is where the combined Austrian and Croatian armies stopped the Ottoman Turks' advance into the western Balkans. I walked a few key places and prayed for the city and the area. I didn't receive any profound revelation, but I did what I needed to do. I put my feet on the ground and claimed it for the Lord, so now He will do what He needs to do.

This past Sunday, I did talk to the man mentioned above that had been a pastor there and he did say that he felt that there was unfinished business there. I am not sure what he meant by that.

One weekend, while Zuzanna was still in the States, Nick Thomson and I went to Gračac for our monthly meetings there. I had made some wooden stakes and wrote scriptures on the sides. Together, with the whole team, we went out to the five entrances of the city and hammered them in the ground next to the city limit signs. We staked out the city for Jesus. This was truly such an encouraging weekend for the Lika team. It was a prophetic act to limit the activity of the enemy. Step-by-step God is helping us take this city.

Nick and I came back Sunday morning. In the evening, we had a Watch Party. Zuzanna and I had been feeling for six months or more that we should start this. What this is: at 10:00 a.m. in Dallas, 5:00 p.m. Zagreb time, UPPERROOM Dallas is live with their Sunday morning service. The idea was to invite people to the prayer room so we could watch it together. So, this was a good time to have the first one because Zuzanna was at UPPERROOM Dallas and was asked to share about the work we do in Croatia and the Balkans. It was really good. We had light food and refreshments. While UPPERROOM Dallas was worshipping, we spent that time just in sharing fellowship with each other. Zuzanna shared and it was good for the team to see the enthusiasm in Dallas for what God is doing in Zagreb, it really was good. Then when Pastor Michael got up to preach, we sat and watched together. We had a few more of these Watch parties, but I guess the time was not ripe for this yet, as it didn't last.

Zuzanna returned from her trip. She had made some interesting connections, but raised no funds. So, now, at this writing, we are in a really tight spot not knowing how we will get to the end of the year. This year—2019—has been already really tough. This is the missionary's life. We depend on God in good times and in bad times, but I am not gonna lie, it can really test our faith sometimes.

We are now faced with the decision to either trim back the ministry, or maybe we are on the verge of a breakthrough. We have momentum going in most areas, so it would be hard to pull back. *Lord, what is it that we need to learn before the breakthrough?* Actually, in both scenarios we need another level of wisdom, strength and confidence in the Lord. There are many plans on the table for the rest of this year, so a cutback would mean many changes. Either way, it is a test of our faith and we need to reject any semblance of defeat.

It is amazing to watch God at work. A few leading evangelical pastors found out that we were working with the Charismatic Catholics, and told Zuzanna that they would like to meet them. We prayed about it for a while, because we wanted to make sure these things are done in the spirit of honor and love. We felt the Lord gave us the green light, and Zuzanna organized a joint gathering in our home. Three predominant evangelical pastors and one missionary represented the evangelical group. Six different leaders from the Charismatic Catholics, the house of prayer leader form Slavonski Brod, also five representatives of the Božja Pobjeda, (God's Victory) worship band attended. It was a remarkable time and we felt that Holy Spirit accomplished what He set out to do in that meeting. Our job now was to get out of the way and let God cultivate the work He has begun.

I must admit that in the past I have had a critical spirit regarding churches established by denomination. It took me over thirty years to get to the point of accepting the fact that God can work through whatever doctrine or church experience one holds as long as the basics of the gospel are in place. We are all on a journey in our Christian development and God will have us in the community that enhances that development best. As it basically says in 1 John, if you believe Jesus has come in the flesh then you are a child of God. My desire is to accept others at the point where God has them presently. I am convinced that I am not able to judge another man's walk with God.

One of the challenges of the mission field is that you miss family back in the States. We were so happy that my sister Glenda, my cousin Cindy, and my son Asa were to visit in May. Glenda and Cindy would stay about two weeks and Asa a month. It was so good to have family here. We took them to see the Plitvice Lakes, to the coast, and then Zuzanna took them to Budapest and then to her birthplace, Subotica. While in Subotica they visited Hajnalka, Zuzanna's youngest sister. They toured the synagogue in Subotica which is an international treasure. It has just been restored. It seats 2,500 and its architecture makes it truly spectacular. It was so good to show Cindy and my sister the ministry the Lord has led us into.

After two weeks, Glenda and Cindy left and Asa stayed another two weeks. The 13th through 17th we went to Vienna to the Awaken Europe event. It was great to see so many Europeans gathered to worship and listen to speakers encourage them. This was amazing to see so many Christians gathered from all parts of Europe. Also, some people came from UPPERROOM Dallas. Our team from Zagreb was Zora, Iva, Zuzanna Asa and I. For some reason, I got sick and had to stay in the apartment and missed some of the sessions. Once back in Zagreb, I went to see my doctor and they really couldn't find the cause of my back pain, but found other things like an enlarged prostate.

The following month, we had a team come to pray in the prayer room from Siberia, Russia. They were traveling around Europe praying in strategic places. They were amazing, real charismatic. We had a special Wednesday night meeting at URGS and they provided live music. Though their style was very unique, we loved to see a different expression of the Body of Christ loving and following Jesus. They are very fervent and they shared with us some of the struggles they face as believers in Russia. They have to meet in the field, due to government harassment, for example. Our home truly is a place of Kingdom people from all over the world coming and going.

······

BASEBALL IN LIKA

We have been faithfully investing into Lika and the city of Gračac, for several years, and the team felt that it was time to begin to step out in a new way. The idea came about to hold a baseball camp. Now, baseball is not very well-known in Croatia. Some missionaries in the past have brought the game into the country and there are a few adult and kids' leagues, but it was definitely unknown to the kids in Lika. We have been planning this event for a while. We learned from our first event that nothing is easy in Lika and we needed to saturate everything we did in prayer.

We couldn't get the soccer field in town, so we decided to make our own field on Vanko's property, where there was plenty of space. It really is a beautiful place with a gorgeous view of the Velebit mountain range, which separates the Adriatic coastline from the inland. The field needed to be cleared of rocks and flattened. Most of Lika is full of random rocks and when you want to work a section of the land, you clear the rocks and stack them at the border of your property line, which ends up making a good fence. There are fences like that which are hundreds of years old. It is amazing to stop and ponder how the previous inhabitants lived, and even some live like that today. The field, the flyers and posters, coaches and all the details were in place, but we really did not know what to expect.

The indigenous people of Lika are not at all open to outsiders and for this reason every move we made was very calculated. We did run into a problem. Pin Oaks Christian Fellowship from Anna, Texas, has been a core supporter of IST and was key in realizing this camp idea. They sent us baseball equipment but it got held up in Croatian customs. But God had a plan. He always has our back.

The 1st Annual Baseball Camp in Gračac turned out awesome. God was touching lives right and left. We ended up with twenty-three children in the camp. The coaches were beyond believable. They all went the extra mile. The head coach, Stefan, was a divine appointment. Remember, earlier I talked about doing a prayer-walk of Sisak? Stefan is part of HisPrint, a ministry that has been doing sports ministry in Eastern Europe for years and he is their main baseball coach. Their headquarters is in Sisak. Of course, I knew nothing about HisPrint at that time. As we put out the request for help with the baseball camp in Gracac, we connected with them. They offered us baseball equipment before we even knew that we would need it, and released Stefan along with multiple coaches to help us.

Nick and I drove down to Sisak to pick up the equipment and it so happened the director of the ministry was there—David was from Houston Texas. He was so gracious toward us and was amazed when I told him I had done a prayer-walk of Sisak a few months earlier. We saw divine appointment after divine appointment. (I love divine appointments. God gets all the glory.)

The summer was pretty busy. We had a team from Burn Europe. They are a group of traveling worshipers and their aim is to go into cities and do extended hours of worship intercession. The team led worship in the prayer room several nights, and we also went out to do street witnessing in the Zrinjevac park. We had many great conversations and many seeds were sown.

Right after the Burn team, we had another team come and they ministered one night in the Upper Room Zagreb. They were Jamaicans from upstate New York. They are traveling around Europe praying for the countries. Who knows how many saints go about doing the Father's business humbly and with no fanfare, spending their own recourses to go and invest into the nations? Zuzanna and I feel humbled to host and facilitate the ones that come through our doors. I love the discipline and dedication of intercessors. One of the ladies on this team was turning seventy-four that day. *Oh, Lord, let me also be a prayer warrior like her when I am 74.*

After our friends from New York left, our new friends and baseball coach Stefan and Ari came up from Sisak to spend a full day with us. They got here just in time to join us for the prayer set. After the set we came home, ate tacos, and played two games of Texas Joker. This morning we had egg tacos which Zuzanna made out of the leftover meat from last night. We talked and talked and played another two games of Texas Joker before they left. Texas Joker is a game that is an adaptation of the Wahoo or Aggravation games. Only about fifty copies were made and then the developers got into a disagreement and quit making them. We have a copy, and it is so much fun to play. Great social entertainment and bonding.

It just amazes me, all these Kingdom people I am getting to meet. God is just so amazing. What great fun we are going to have in heaven.

PART SIX

SABBATICAL

Chapter Eighteen

In February, when we had our pastoral visit from UPPERROOM, it was strongly suggested that we take an extended Sabbatical since we have been on the field for over five years now. We were so happy to hear this suggestion and honestly really needed it. The team suggested six months, but we felt like four months was all we could do since it was going to be the first time we would leave the team for any extended period of time. So, Joanna, the missions director and an IST board member, helped set everything up and in mid-August the time came for us to head to the States.

We made it to Dallas. As usual, Joy picked us up. We love that we always get to see her whenever we come. We spent the first night with her, and the next day we went to meet the people who are letting us stay in their tiny house. Their names are Daniel and Alana. We met with them and they showed us the things we needed to do to take care of the house. Quite a remarkable tiny house it was. Daniel and a friend built it. It is basically the size of a cargo container. The great thing about it is that it is within walking distance of UPPERROOM. Also, we have their car to use which is also a great blessing. The first week was us adjusting to jet lag. From Day One, we spent many hours at UPPERROOM in the prayer sets. This is what satisfies our soul. We are so grateful for this time to disconnect and get refilled.

During our second week in America, we went to Lubbock to visit the Boyds, who are the founders of Prepare International. We spent two nights with them and met with the mission director at their church, Church on the Rock. The meeting with the director felt very good. It was so very encouraging to see that in this era when many are distancing themselves from supporting missionaries to foreign fields, Church on the Rock in Lubbock is a church which is still placing a strong priority on missions. We planned to return for a follow-up visit in the Spring of 2020, but COVID-19 changed so many things.

We came back to Dallas and Sunday we went to Pin Oaks Christian Fellowship in Anna, Texas. We shared in both services. We sure do love the folks at Pin Oaks They have believed in us pretty much from the start. Our son Asa went with us and then we went to the 5 p.m. service at UPPERROOM – Frisco.

One of the really nice benefits of being home for a sabbatical is that we get to see our children. About a month into our time in the United States, we went to see our son Gordon and his family in Las Vegas. It was a good time staying at Gordon and Lauren's. The girls are growing and we were there for Dakota's birthday. She turned two. Cheyenne is a bundle of energy and very smart. Koda (Dakota's nickname) is just in that real loving age. Their characters are so different. At times like this we realize that a true sacrifice of our 'yes' to God is that we miss so much of our grandchildren's growth and we are just not able to be so involved with them as normal grandparents can.

One day we were in the prayer room at UPPERROOM Dallas and there was a time when prayer was offered in the room and I acknowledged a need for physical healing. A man came over and prayed for me and then afterward we talked. I told him we were missionaries. He went back to his seat but after the prayer time he came over and handed us three hundred dollars. He said he wanted to give into our ministry and he felt like it was seed money for three things. Then Zuzanna said what she thought the three things were for us: 1) that the house of prayer in Zagreb will go to another level; 2) there will be enough money come in to secure a place in Gračac for the church-plant to meet; and 3) that we will be financially secure for another year.

The gentleman's name is Sam and he had another gentleman with him named Jim. They came down from Arkansas the day before to spend time in the prayer room and were leaving right after that prayer-set to go back. He also said he had three businesses and the $300 were seeds being sown from those businesses. Now here is the amazing part. Later that evening, we got a message from Sam asking us to call him. So, we called and he was so excited. As he and Jim left us, he was walking out of the building and he got a call from his partner of one of his businesses and the partner said they had just gotten a call from Amazon asking them to bid on a construction job. We acknowledged this was the hand of God in response to his seed faith.

Friday morning, we met with Joanna (UR missions leader) and Traes (UR worship leader) to plan their next trip to Croatia in March 2020. Part of their ministry was to include serving as worship leaders for the Vatra Conference in Slovonski Brod, which is organized by the charismatic Catholics. (The Vatra conference ended up being canceled because of Covid-19 .

One Friday evening, we went to Sandi's house for a Shabbat (the Jewish Day of Rest), and saw many former Shady Grovers there. This was a good time of reconnecting with Polly, Rocky and Margaret, Michael, Bernie, Sarah, Rob, and others.

Then the following night we went to Prayer Mountain (the Mountain Creek area of Dallas) for a small meeting where there were some other Shady Grove friends of ours. Asa was with us, too. Our friend Norm had a powerful word for us of assurance of provision and increase for the ministry in Croatia. God sure does know how to put wind in our sails. This word truly encouraged us.

We also were able to visit Pastor Michael and Lorisa's for dinner. This was very special for us. It was such a relaxed and intimate time in their home and we got to really share our hearts with one another. We so value their leadership and the DNA of UPPERROOM, which they are stewarding. They are such heroes of the faith. We love them so much. We really wish we could know them better, but this is part of the cost of doing missions overseas. You don't have the time to develop deep friendships with people back in America. We are just not in the States much.

Even though we are on a sabbatical, we still have to do some fundraising for next year. We had a banquet which was at the UPPERROOM Overflow room. Zuzanna and I shared the vision for Croatia. Peter Louis was our main speaker and Traes was the moderator. Once again, we saw God's faithfulness as the people who attended were so generous to sow into the work in Croatia. We continue to be amazed at how God keeps taking care of us and the work that He has led us to.

After the banquet we went to Denver to spend a month or so at the UPPERROOM there. Sean picked us up at the airport. It was so good to see him. He took us to where we are staying, with Bradley and Savannah. We got to really know and love this family and their precious kids.

Being in Denver was a lot of fun. We went to Estes Park and to the Rocky Mountain National Park. Estes Park is an amazing little city full of tourists. It was unique in many ways. The Rocky Mountains are beautiful and huge, so we only saw a portion of the park. I bought a National Park pass that is good in any national park in America for a year. The senior pass only cost twenty dollars and I can take one other person with me. I hope we get to use this more. Zuzanna and I talked about doing more of this in the future; to visit national parks when we are stateside. It is so rejuvenating to see God's beautiful creation.

We also wanted to take a road trip to Park City, Utah. We left Denver on a Thursday morning and drove for about nine hours across beautiful Colorado, on into Utah and across the Rocky Mountains. We went to see Asa's friends of several years. They have a home church, and they are really special people. They treated us special and in their Friday evening Shabbat we were able to share about the work in Croatia. There was some ministry time and the Lord showed up to minister to all of us. The believers there took up an offering and blessed us so very generously.

Saturday, about noon, we started back and took a different route back to Denver.

The next day we visited a church in Colorado Springs where Don and Michelle Patterson are the pastors. We shared in their service and had chili with the church members afterward. Then we went for coffee with Don and Michelle. We talked and talked and didn't want to leave. There was such fellowship between us. We made it back to Denver in time for church at UPPERROOM Denver. Wintertime in Denver means snow. The next few days we got some heavy snow, about eight to ten inches. We moved to Don and Kathy's for a week. They really have a lovely home in Littleton, a suburb of Denver. They are elders at the church and it was really nice to get to know them a bit. Zuzanna loved spending time with Kathy.

Jennie Fitzgerald begged Zuzanna for us to come and stay a week with them, so we agreed. We so deeply love this family and they have visited us twice in Croatia, leaving a real mark on our community there. The Fitzgeralds have a warm home in Golden, Colorado. It is nice to spend time with friends who love us and appreciate the ministry we do. Also, we are making new friends in Denver.

Last Monday, the Fitzgeralds treated us to an overnight stay at Glen Eyrie Castle, a resort area next to Garden of the Gods in Colorado Springs. The resort was really beautiful, five-star accommodations. But something happened before we got there. We decided to go to the Garden of the Gods before checking into the resort. While there, I slipped on some ice and fell flat on my back. It knocked the breath out of me and Zuzanna had to help me up. I was hurting really bad. We went on to the Glen Eyrie and checked in, but I was really hurting. With only my Medicare coverage, which we never really used before, we decided to see what would happen with the pain, rather than going to a hospital. Well, the pain continued. It was really hard to bend over. I had cracked a rib once before and all you can do is be patient while it heals. It looked like this was the same situation.

Well, it was time to get back to Texas. We have had such a restful sabbatical and time was approaching for us to return to Zagreb. We got to stay at Elias' house in the Modern Day mission suite. Over the last couple years, we have stayed there a few times and what a blessing. Elias and the Modern Day team provide such a valuable service to missionaries. When Shady Grove merged with Gateway, Modern Day stepped in and provided a real net for all of us missionaries. Not only to help process our finances, but also they have been so helpful in many other ways. We even got a visit from Elias one year in Croatia. Truly, God raised up Elias Rayes and his team for such a time as this.

Before returning to Croatia, we went to Los Angeles for Thanksgiving. Joy flew with us and Asa flew in on the 27th. We stayed at Gordon's in-laws (Lauren's parents) for five days. We as a family were all together for the first time in five years. It was more of a family-together-time rather than a tourist time in Los Angeles. It was tight but we were happy to be together.

Lauren's parents, Diane and Mark, are so kind and love our son Gordon. And I must add here that they are such wonderful grandparents to our granddaughters, which is gratifying since we can't be with them nearly as much. We are thankful to them because this was a true sacrifice for them to let us stay with them. We then returned to Texas where we stayed with Joy until we flew back to Croatia a few days later.

• • • • • •

BACK IN ZAGREB

Back in Zagreb at last. We are so thankful for the time of rest in the States, but Zagreb is our home and we quickly got back into the joy of serving in the prayer room. It was December, which meant that Zuzanna quickly joined the planning team for the Advent event with the seventeen-plus pastors and several NGOs. Unity efforts seemed to be moving forward in Zagreb in this season and it was a joy for Zuzanna to serve on this team of key leaders from Zagreb.

We went to Subotica for Christmas and stayed a few extra days. While we were there we went to see the Sabos. Viktor had prostate cancer so it was good to encourage him. He had been through some bad times this past year. These troubles have led them into a deeper walk with the Lord. We prayed for grace and healing for Viktor. We sure do love this man and his family. What a legacy and a life lived for the Kingdom.

PART SEVEN

NEW YEAR, NEW DECADE

Chapter Nineteen

We entered into 2020 full speed and with new energy. There was a real momentum not only in Zagreb but in Lika also. The house in the city of Gračac that the IST team has spent years praying in became available as the family renting it has moved out. We had gone to visit Vanko and Blanka, and as we brainstormed, the team had the idea to rent that house since it was still available. So Vanko contacted the owner and it was done. We could still continue to meet there for our monthly meetings and Vanko and family could stay there every time they go to Gračac to work on their house. Also, we now had a base for outreaches such as the baseball camp, etc. This is a big step forward in Gračac for ministry. We have been consistent for three years to pray and believe for a breakthrough.

With all the momentum, it was past time for us to have help. Andrea has been a faithful young prayer leader who saw Jesus do so much in her life through the prayer room. She has become such a faithful helper to Zuzanna, and we brought her on, working part-time as the IST assistant. We believed this would be an awesome year for IST and the prayer room (Upper Room Zagreb).

Zuzanna and I went on a 21-day fast. She did water only and I was on a soup fast. We were feeling overwhelmed by His trust and really inadequate at the same time for what was to come. This fast was really taking us into deeper communion and trust that Jesus was in control.

It was time to do another Watch Party at the Upper Room Zagreb. We had nine people. The watch party consisted of watching UPPER-ROOM Dallas. The objective was to reach out to the English-speaking community of Zagreb and to provide a taste of the new wine skin that UPPERROOM carries. It went really well, although a different format than what people are used to. Sort of like a home-group and a church service mixed. The message was Kevin Tipps speaking on humility. Everyone was ministered to and at the end we had discussion time about the message. It was so encouraging to see that people really listened and had meaningful takeaways.

There are some factors involved in these watch parties. One is that there desperately needs to be what we call a "new wine skin" here in the Balkans. We believe this to mean a fresh way of doing and living in church community. The millennials and Gen Z simply are not finding the present Balkan church relevant to their lives and, for the most part, those generations are missing from the Protestant churches altogether. We personally feel that our two years at UPPERROOM Dallas, before we came to Croatia, were meant to see a new wine skin up close. We believe these watch parties may be a step toward raising up this new wine skin in the Balkans and Zagreb is a great testing ground. This is why we believe God brought us to that city.

There is another factor here also. For the past two years, we have been getting requests from foreign Christians here in Zagreb to start an international church; that is, basically an English-speaking church. Most large cities in Europe have one or more international congregations. So, we felt that maybe the Lord wanted to use an international type of church to bring in a new wine skin. Now we know, an international church will be labeled "too American" or "British." There is an element in the Protestant churches in the region that is critical of foreign church expressions, especially the American expression. If you take a close look, however, they are already modeling American churches of fifty years ago. The fact is that western churches have led the way in many ways for maybe the last one hundred years. I definitely believe that the typical American church has missed the mark in many areas, but one of the things we love about the UPPERROOM is that it has recognized some of those shortcomings and has really tried to cultivate a different culture, a different DNA. A new wine skin.

......

SOFIA, BULGARIA

In early February of 2020, we drove down to Sofia, Bulgaria, for the Annual Balkan Networks meeting. This is a meeting we have with spiritual leaders from some of the Balkan countries once a year. We sort of get a feel of what God is doing throughout the Balkans, and we also have a time of encouraging one another and fellowship. This is so helpful because ministry in foreign lands can be so very lonely. The meetings went great. Much encouraging, praying and prophesying over each other too. We even celebrated Zuzanna's birthday.

After long hours of meeting on Saturday, February 8th (Zuzanna's birthday), we went out to eat. When we came out of the restaurant to go to our hotel, we found that our car had been stolen. We went to the police to report it, filled out all the paperwork, and I guess the police put out a search alert. They told us that this happens a lot to foreigners visiting the country. They told us that the thieves would contact us asking for ransom to get our car back.

Shock and disbelief really hit both of us and all our Balkan Network friends as they were leaving for their respective countries while we had to extend our stay in the hotel. On December 31, 2019, Zuzanna received a very clear word from the Lord that at the end of 2020, nothing would be the same as we knew it. I don't think we realized at this time that this was the beginning of the year that would fundamentally change not only *our* lives, but the world.

Sunday morning, we were attending the host church and it so happened that a former criminal was also there. He had recently become a believer so the pastor said we should talk to him. The fellow said he would check with his old friends to see if they knew of the car and who had it. Sure enough, before the day was over, he got back with us and said he found who had our car and that he could negotiate for us. He said they wanted 4,000€, he would be the middle man, and we were not to go to the police. It turns out they were the Bulgarian mafia.

Our minds were racing. It is quite a humbling experience to face your own heart in such a situation. What would you do? At first, we were just thinking we wanted the car back and were maybe willing to pay the ransom. God is so gracious when we are foolish and if we are listening, He will use what He can to get our attention. By now it was late at night and such a cold, wintry day, with only the snow to illuminate the darkness. We walked from our hotel room to three different ATMs. Two were out of order and the third would only give us fifty dollars.

At this point, Zuzanna said we needed more wisdom from our spiritual leaders. There had to be a reason why we couldn't get to the funds. We tried contacting the chairman of IST board, but he was not available. We did finally get ahold of Joanna, our UPPERROOM missions director. She said she would get some of the UPPERROOM leaders together to talk and pray about our situation. Once we got off the phone with Joanna, we began to look at the spiritual ramifications.

By not getting the car back, the ministry would be hurt in many ways. Our travel would be minimized, it would take longer to get places, and it would be more expensive. We would also have to try and raise money to buy another car, just at the time we are trying to raise money for the property in Gračac. The real spiritual ramifications, however, are far more important. We would be supporting the corruption we have been praying that God would expose and pull down in the Balkans.

By getting the car back, much of the above consequences would be minimized. A real problem would be interacting with the Bulgarian police. We would have to tell the police we just found it on the side of the road or that we had parked it in another place and had forgot. These would be outright lies. The more we thought about all this, the more we knew we just could not live with this. Another thing to consider was the newly saved middle man. What kind of example would that be if we handled this the same way that the world does? We would not want this situation to cause him to be hurt or take him back into that lifestyle.

We came to the realization this was a profound test and we wanted to pass it in a pure and spotless way. In the meantime, we also got a call back form Gary, our chairman, and he absolutely agreed that we should not negotiate with the mafia.

We bought airline tickets and flew home the next day. The reality of the situation hit us hard. Leaving Bulgaria without our car, the worst thing was the loss of our Bibles and all the notes our Bibles contained. It was so hard to believe this had happened, but we knew we were doing the right thing. Now we were to wait to see how our Father in heaven would work this out for our good. We felt it our pleasure to suffer this setback because we were coming in the opposite-spirit to combat crime and corruption, which are so rampant and such a stronghold in the Balkans.

Let me interject what I felt God was speaking to me at the Balkan Networks meeting. I was stirred to pray that God would raise up an apostolic/prophetic group in the Balkans that will make covenant with each other to identify and raise up anointed evangelists, teachers and pastors. These would be men and women that have been tested by fire and walk in their office with power. These would be men and women that do not fight against flesh and blood but know how to fight along with the armies of heaven to bring forth God's glory. They can also be trusted with the finances of the Kingdom. They will be willing to suffer so the Kingdom can be established on earth.

PART EIGHT

TRAPPED IN AMERICA — AGAIN

Chapter Twenty

Here was a new decade and our world unraveling as we knew it.

Things began happening to me that I did not plan for. My left hand was getting worse. There was the loss of coordination and shrinking muscles. So, we scheduled an appointment with a specialist to have it checked out. They determined it was not carpal tunnel, but nerve-related. So, I was scheduled to have an MRI. Well, while in the MRI machine, I had a panic attack. This was really strange because I know of no other time that I have had a panic attack. Loss of breath and visible shaking. I thought it was claustrophobia at the time. The MRI was not completed. We had to schedule another time for the MRI but I just could not do it. So, I needed to do it, but when and how? Zuzanna found another place here in Zagreb that seemed to have a more modern and less-confining machine. Lord, I needed courage.

I felt that this was an attack of fear from the enemy. One of the alarming things about this was that I couldn't even pray in the spirit. Would I be able to stand in the strength of the Lord? *Lord, would you just heal me?* The following Thursday evening, in the prayer set, I was really being attacked by fear. A dear sister who knew nothing about my situation asked to pray for me. God was speaking through her and she identified the fear and prayed for confidence and assurance. She spoke of me being prepared for another level of authority in the Kingdom, but at the same time she said that it was time for me to get out of the battle. I knew this was a word from the Lord, but what did all this mean?

Another physical problem was my breathing. I couldn't take deep breaths. This was affecting my energy level, causing light dizziness, and sometimes even mental confusion. We got an x-ray of my lungs, but it revealed nothing. Something was restricting my breathing. With the deterioration of my hand, shallow breathing and the panic attack, I was asking the Lord what was going on. Were these issues going to lead to Him taking me home to be with Him, or was I being tested in preparation for a greater anointing here on earth? Now, I was not even sure I had the theology right on all this. *Lord, I know I seriously need Your help.*

Corona virus, wow! In early March, things started to look serious as this pandemic was getting out of control. It pressed the whole world into fear. Gatherings were being restricted at that time to one hundred or less. All churches were beginning to go to streaming only. We felt that for now we needed to continue having sets but we decided to cut back on how many prayer sets we would have each week. Rather than five we were going to trim down to three and then a Saturday Upper Room Watch Party.

It quickly became obvious that this would be a paradigm shift for the whole world. Something like 9-11 was or even bigger. Either way, the thing for the Church to do right now was not let fear get a foothold. Some immediate questions that emerged were, how do we continue to be Christlike under a new paradigm? How will we minister to others in a world where nearness and touch are suspect?

In March, we had a team scheduled to come from Dallas. This was to be a large leap forward, as the team was to lead worship at the Vatra conference organized by our Charismatic Catholic friends. Vatra was a high-profile conference and this was a big, bold move by them and us to publicly do an event together. We were really excited about this move. Also, the team was going to spend a lot of quality time with our leaders, working to develop them and really invest in them. As the whole world was going to lock-down, of course they had to cancel the trip. We were so very sad, and wondered where all this was going.

By March 22, the city was in lock-down due to Corona. A little after six a.m., we woke up and the house was violently shaking. It was clear we were having an earthquake. As soon as there was a pause, we got our clothes on and went outside. This was a 5.5 with the epicenter just a few short miles from us. There were some tremors and then about thirty minutes later, another 5.0 quake. Over about an hour-and-a-half time period there were three quakes and several tremors.

We finally went back inside to check the damage. We were very thankful to be in a building that was built to withstand a 7.5 earthquake; nevertheless, there was still plenty of damage. All the walls cracked and upstairs in the old prayer room the end walls looked really bad. There was broken glass and more damage in the kitchen. The roof sustained some damage and the whole building, which is on a mountainside, had tilted forward about a half-inch. We had never been in an earthquake before, so this was quite the experience. There was massive damage in the city where poorly maintained old buildings just collapsed or became unlivable. We didn't know much yet, but we knew that this tragedy would have long-lasting consequences on this city and nation.

Some friends from the Croatian coast called to see if we were okay. On the news, they had said they predicted another aftershock in a couple of days. These friends suggested we come and stay in their Airbnb apartment, which was empty this time of year. We discussed this with our assistant Andreja, and decided that we should do that.

After we got back from Bulgaria, Joanna started a fundraiser to replace our car, but Zuzanna wanted to go to Germany to purchase a car. Now, due to Covid, this was not going to happen just now. As soon as we got back from Bulgaria, I had all those medical issues, so Zuzanna went out and got an old beat-up car that was not really safe for highways but could get us to the doctors and around town. So, we had no choice but to take little Herby (Andrea named it that and it stuck) and, driving under sixty miles per hour, we made it down to the Airbnb in Primošten.

Once we arrived, we heard on the news that due to the virus, everyone trying to leave the city of Zagreb was stopped and not allowed due to the city being locked down as a result of Covid. The angels must have hidden us, because no one stopped us. Because we came from a city that was in lock-down, we had to self-quarantine in Primošten. That meant staying in the apartment and not going to the beach.

Our landlord in Zagreb went to look at the damage in the house and he told us that structurally the building was stable and therefore we could return. We were told we would have to wait for a long time for any repairs as it was impossible to get any contractors. We stayed in the Airbnb for five days and then returned to Zagreb, where Zuzanna and Andrea began the task of cleaning up the mess in the apartment.

This corona virus thing was getting to be crazy; a life changer. I guess the government can enact emergency measures for situations like this, but it sure limits freedom. It was a ministry changer. We had to start thinking outside of the box. *God, what are we to do?*

In April, we were still in stay-at-home mode, by order of the Croatian government. Many spontaneous groups started Zoom prayer meetings and it was really invigorating to see the Body of Christ stepping up to the challenges of this situation. The precious believers who attended Upper Room Zagreb were going through all sorts of challenges. Families suddenly had to homeschool as schools were in lock-down and children had to Zoom into class. This brought on such stress to so many.

We knew that we had to figure out some way to connect with our people, and we did. The city restriction was that no more than five people could gather at a time. So we made a schedule and every night of the week and sometimes several times per day, we met with people one on one. Everyone was on a schedule and each week we would see them at the same time. We prayed with them and ministered to their needs in whatever way they needed it. This worked well for our small community and I would say that it was a lifeline for so many in those hardest days. As we look back, we see this time as a great deepening of relationships and openness by everyone. What the enemy meant for evil, God turned into good.

By the beginning of May, the Croatian government started to ease up some, and they allowed for ten people to meet. Churches started gathering again and so did we. I remember our first prayer set we had ten adults. Marko and Sara led worship and it was powerful. We were all so happy to be together once again.

It has now been three months since the world has changed due to this virus and many, including myself, really have begun to question some things concerning the lock-down and the way governments were handling this whole thing. I was trying to understand what was happening in the spiritual realm. I knew that principalities have been operating in this manner since being kicked out of heaven. Usually, they would do their work behind the scenes, but if you understand their ways of operating, this pandemic was their opportunity to influence governments.

I know one thing. God is greater. Although the Bible says God caused plagues and pestilences to come upon lands as punishments, instead of 'caused,' I really like to think of it as 'allowed'. Sometimes God has to lift off His protective hand and let the principalities wreak havoc, because essentially the nation or nations brought it on themselves. It was a consequence of their actions. Sometimes God has to let trouble come just so men can see their sins and hopefully repent so His blessings can be reinstated. (That is *my* theology. You don't have to agree.)

Either way, God was waking people up and we began to see signs that this could possibly open the wells of revival. One of the positive things we were beginning to see was that as shelter-in-place was prolonged, families were having to face relationship issues and parents and children were beginning to spend more quality time together. Now, we also saw the negative side of this as, of course, many did not handle it right and allowed stress and dysfunction to take them deeper.

We decided we would have a worship night on Pentecost, June 31, at the Upper Room. We used the downstairs, in the Agape church space. Maybe about fifty people came. Marko organized a band and they were really good. We reversed the service with the message first and then a long time of worship. The objective was to let the message build up to the worship time, not the traditional way. The Lord gave a word to Zuzanna about the Laodicean church in the book of Revelations. I think she and Darija spent ten days beforehand fasting and praying for the event.

But then the strangest thing happened on the day of the meeting. On the way to the building, Zuzanna was driving, and suddenly she felt sick and pulled over. As she got out of the car, she fainted, collapsing to the ground. Andrea and I helped her up and she fainted again. What was so very strange was that Zuzanna is never sick and she has not fainted since she was pregnant. We really felt that it was a spiritual attack because of the word of the Lord she was to bring. She was determined to share the word anyway and it was the right word. At the end, we had a time of praying for those who wanted to be filled with the Holy Spirit. Many came forward for various prayer needs and the Holy Spirit was working.

Meanwhile, my health was not getting any better. In fact, my breathing was getting worst, my energy was real low, and I was actually starting to have no appetite. Although I was still eating, I was beginning to lose a lot of weight. In three months, I lost thirty pounds. People have been praying for me everywhere I go. Also, the muscle deterioration in my hands has advanced some.

Zuzanna found another clinic where I could get an MRI done privately, and they positioned me at an incline so that I could still breathe. The MRI was successful and it was showing a neurological problem, possibly a pinched nerve in my spine that was thought to be causing the problems I was experiencing. Now, in Croatia at this time, to get a neurosurgeon appointment you would be having to wait many months, which we did not have. A friend from the Upper

Room Zagreb, who worked at one of the hospitals in town, was able to get a neurosurgeon to take a look at the results of the MRI without an appointment. He very graciously did, and advised us that without examining me personally, it really looked like a pinched nerve, and I would need surgery. Right away he let us know that the wait for surgery was two-plus years.

We knew that this meant we had to return to the United States, because the progression of whatever was going on with me could not wait two years, and besides, if I was going to have spinal surgery, I probably wanted that done in the U.S. So, even while Zuzanna was organizing the Pentecost event, which we felt really strongly from the Lord that we were supposed to do, she was also making plans for us to go back to Texas so we could see doctors there. I have not been to a doctor in the U.S. in the seven years that we have lived in Croatia. Zuzanna was navigating through a lot to get everything set up ahead of time. Two days after the Day of Pentecost, we landed in Dallas.

We were so hungry to be around our church family that with jet lag, sickness and all, the day after we landed we went to the prayer set at UPPERROOM. Pastor Michael and some of the elders prayed over us. We felt comforted and loved.

Meanwhile, my breathing and sleeping problems were getting worse; not only from jet lag, but the constant shortness of breath. Thursday, I had to be taken to the ER at Grapevine Baylor. I was really struggling with my breathing. They ran some tests on me and determined all my vitals were fine and I had to go to my primary physician. I came back to Joy's but struggled to get to sleep. Utterly exhausted, I finally slept some. In the following days, I was feeling a little better. I truly felt the prayers of the saints. The Body of Christ is a powerful spiritual force.

Now let me give a bit of a back story. When we moved to Croatia in 2013, Joy had just graduated from high school and was starting college. She did not want to move to Croatia with us, and so we wanted her to live with a family for at least the first year. One of her friends from school had an amazing family. They were the Sharps. Kelly and Dr. Rebecca Sharp were truly a loving couple who loved Jesus and loved young people. We will be forever thankful to them for taking in Joy and allowing her to live with them through a really challenging and changing time in her life.

Dr. Sharp became my primary doctor and after our first visit she put a plan of action in place. The following week was filled with appointment after appointment, trying to get to the bottom of what was happening with my health.

• • • • • •

THE DIAGNOSIS

Two weeks after our arrival in the U.S., we had our first neurologist appointment. We didn't expect much from this appointment, because by now our main focus had become my shallow breathing and we realized that no surgery could be done if I can't breathe normally. I don't think we will ever forget the little austere room that we were placed in while we waited for the neurologist to come in. He had a very—shall we say—different personality. He asked me two questions only, and then asked if we have ever heard of Lou Gehrig's or the ALS disease. Honestly, we knew very little of it, though we knew it was serious, but didn't really know anything else. He said he believed that all the symptoms I had were an indication of ALS. This included my breathing also. In retrospect, I can understand the doctor's strange behavior in the room; probably not easy to deliver such news.

In regard to this bad news, I had two remembrances from my heart healing in 2014. First, I was misdiagnosed as having pneumonia (from the looks of it, this happened again by the Croatian doctor), but it ended up being congestive heart disease. Second, the doctors said it would never heal. Once an enlarged heart, it never heals. They told me I could live with that heart condition for the rest of my life, and would need to remain on medication. I remember that the biggest hindrance at the time was a lack of strength. I had many conversations with the Lord about this at that time, but promised Him that I would serve Him even in my lack of strength. I would do what I could do with the strength I had. It was two things: an initial misdiagnosis and that it was incurable. What will God do? Will I be able to serve Him with this disease or will He heal me?

There was another remarkable thing that happened. From that neurologist appointment we were heading to a memorial service of a dear friend, Calvin McCrary, who had passed away on Monday June 15th. Calvin and Karen McCrary have been giving to our work for years. The memorial service was at the Gateway Grand Prairie campus. Many former Shady Grove members attended, so it was good to see them. Calvin was a remarkable man and the testimonies of his life went on and on. Like at most memorial services, we went filing by to give our condolences to the family.

Zuzanna went before me and told Karen, the widow, of the news we had just received that most likely I had ALS. When I got to Karen, she started consoling me by praying for me. This is the first time I have been to a memorial service or funeral and had the grieving widow pray for me. Then as I walked over to the side, Zuzanna had assembled many of our friends and former elders to pray for me. They sat me down and prayed some powerful prayers. Words were given that God is not finished with me. Amen! This was great encouragement. God is amazing. He is excellent in how He works.

We really had no idea what ALS was until we got home and Zuzanna started Googling it. That was probably not such a good idea: Terminal disease… No cure… full paralysis… Shock… Disbelief…

The next few days were a blur. I decided that the way for me to keep my eyes on the Lord was that I did not want to know anything except what I really had to about ALS. Zuzanna agreed to respect that, even though she would have to learn about it in order to help me navigate through the process. I think we all had waves of emotions and were trying to deal with them in our own way. Father's Day was that weekend, and all three of the children came into town to see us, and Gordon brought Cheyenne also. God set this up for us. This was such a gift to have us all together so we could begin to process the information and each our feelings. Family is such a gift of God.

I am very thankful for my spiritual family also. Brian Benchley from the Balkan Networks, who lives in Macedonia, put together a series of prayer zoom calls and forty days of fasting for my health. Many friends from Australia to Canada, from Argentina to Siberia, joined the calls. I was amazed at the dedication from those who prayed and sent messages.

We had several ALS doctor visits and more tests. Not only is ALS incurable at this time, but there is no test which says you have ALS. This means that even though the doctors were pretty sure that it was ALS, the potential for many diseases had to be eliminated before an official diagnosis could be given. The official diagnosis of ALS was finally given July 15, 2020.

On the heels of all this, I had my 70th birthday. I am in no hurry to go to heaven, but I wonder how many more years I have here on earth. I look at it like this: Since we are going to be in Heaven for eternity, why not stay here longer. I realized that with this ALS, only God knew. I was believing for healing because I knew this was an attack of the enemy. I just want to see Jesus glorified in the Balkans.

At last, I finished all my appointments and Dr. Maria Phillip became my ALS doctor going forward. I was now using an in-home BiPAP ventilator, which was helping me sleep better, and Dr. Phillip said that I could still travel for a time and that I should take advantage of what strength I had. This was great news, because we thought we could not go back at all. Zuzanna got us tickets and we arrived the last week of August in Zagreb.

We arrived to a mess…After the earthquakes in Zagreb, it was very hard to find contractors and the landlord promised he would get it all fixed before we got back. Well, let's just say that the apartment looked like a construction zone when we walked in. Had we known this, we would have gotten a hotel. Zuzanna almost had Saša take us back to the airport. She was pretty upset. We had been awake for over twenty-four hours and now had no bed to lie down in and I was very weak. Zuzanna got it all worked out with the workers and a few days later we had the entire Upper Room team come to help deep clean our apartment. We just love these faithful friends!

· · · · · ·

OSKAR AND MAARIT

I need to backtrack a little here. I want to brag about the faithfulness of God. A couple of years ago, a connection happened with the leaders of one of the Burn teams that came to Zagreb. (A Burn Team is a group of musicians and singers that have a van and they travel from city to city leading worship in whatever venue they can set up or they are invited to.) Zuzanna began to share with her that we really needed Levites/Worship leaders. She spoke with one couple from Sweden who she felt was the right couple, but they felt it was not the right time. Then, in April of 2020, two years after the initial conversations, Oskar and Maarit Lindwall, contacted us. This was amazing, because we were getting ready to come to the U.S. for my medical needs, and we were really praying for someone who could pick up the baton at least for a season and run with it. So Zuzanna was corresponding with them and they agreed to come in September for one month and see how the Lord leads beyond that.

We were full of anticipation to welcome Oskar and Maarit, at the beginning of September. At the same time, we had another intern scheduled to spend a month with us, Bianka Domajnko, a German missionary, to Kosovo. The Lord brought her to us to serve in the prayer room for a month, and then a week later her friend from

Finland, Marika Lähteenmäki, joined us as well. It was a delight to have them and it felt so wonderful to have the apartment full of life again. All four served in the prayer room and it was a real boost to our team as well. We have seen over and over again God using the different cultures and expressions. God created cultures and people with individuality and whenever we can be united around worship, it is so powerful. At the end of the one-month trial, we just knew Oskar and Maarit were sent by God, and they felt led to give us a one-year commitment. This was yet another sign to us of God's faithfulness and proof that the Upper Room Zagreb was His doing and He would provide the people to lead it in every season.

Things were really coming alive in the prayer room and God was adding to our numbers as well. His presence was so real and every set was so unique. We saw God really work in hearts. We just never knew what to expect. He always showed up. We were working with Oskar and Maarit to prepare them for when we departed. We planned on leaving in January of 2021.

Then, in November, both Zuzanna and I contracted Covid. This was not good news for me, because of my respiratory issues already from ALS. How this all played out was yet further proof that if we seek first His Kingdom and His righteousness, He will add all we need for us. We had Oskar and Maarit living with us who had already had Covid earlier that year, and so they cared for us.

I was instructed by Dr. Sharp to stay on the BiPAP ventilator as close to 24/7 as I could and, for the most part, I had a lighter version of the virus than Zuzanna. The last three days were very hard and dangerous, but in the end we got better. Even so, my ALS has progressed faster and we made the decision that we needed to get back to the States. The main concern was my ability to withstand the seventeen or so hours' flight. At first, we thought we would go to the U.S., get all the equipment like a power chair, Eye Gaze, and other things, and then we would return to Zagreb. So, we planned on just staying in the States for six months or so.

After getting through the virus, given my progression, it became a foregone conclusion that unless God healed me, we were destined to live in America for the remainder of my life. I had to be the saddest person in the world—Trapped in America once again.

And here is the strangest thing on top of it all. After Zuzanna purchased the tickets in a rush, we realized that it was seven years to the day that we landed in Zagreb and when we were returning to the States. So peculiar that it was the same day, December 14th, that we departed seven years later.

God is so good, I just have to brag about Him again. When I got diagnosed with ALS, as Zuzanna was doing research, we knew that she would need help caring for me as things progressed. There was a special young lady, Ksenija, at the Zagreb Upper Room, who was a nurse with lots of experience and Zuzanna early on thought she would be the person we should hire. The interesting thing was that God had been speaking to her as well about a big change coming to her as well. I am amazed not only that God had prepared her ahead of time, but that He provided the funds to bring her on as my caretaker and nurse. She would travel with us and live with us for many months. Ksenija was such a delight, and our family will always be so very thankful that she helped care for me even though it was trying at times.

Our first month in Dallas was such a blur. We were staying in an Airbnb while Zuzanna was trying to secure living arrangements and resettle us. We were all just trying to cope with the changes which were suddenly forced upon us. We definitely did not want to be in Dallas. We wanted to be back with our beloved team in Zagreb.

Meanwhile, my ALS was getting worse. One morning we were at a prayer set and while trying to write down some notes, I discovered that I can no longer grip a pencil. This made me cry. I have loved writing in my little notebook things the Lord would show me. I would have to start taking my tablet to the prayer room from now on (as long as my fingers will still punch keys).

God is awesome. My life verse especially in my later years has been "Seek first the Kingdom of God and His righteousness and all these things will be added unto you" Matt. 6:33. I have seen God add unto me over and over again when I would spend my time and focus seeking Him. Well, He did it again.

David and Theresa Cantwell, old friends from Shady Grove Church, heard about our situation and offered us and Ksenija accommodations in their home in Arlington. ALS is labeled by medical experts as the worse disease in the world, and we really did not want to present such a burden on the Cantwells, so we had hoped to purchase a home. This was not to be. Our modest missionary income, coupled with a huge rise in housing prices, was not realistic. We love it when God guides us with open doors and the forward momentum is great. But then, there are times when God guides us by shutting doors. This one is not fun and can be so disappointing. Looking back, though, concerning buying a house or even renting a place, we were so thankful that in His infinite wisdom God shut these doors.

The Cantwells insisted that we stay with them throughout the duration of my illness, and are real happy that we are living with them. We are really so amazed. Not many people would not only house a terminally ill patient, but then give us their master bedroom and let us remodel the bathroom and a few other changes in order to make the home wheelchair-accessible.

At this time, our future is unclear. ALS continues relentlessly to take over my physical body…I still have some good days among the many bad days. You never think of just how your body depends on muscles for basic functions. Slowly, I am losing the use of my extremities and also breathing, swallowing, and speech. My mind is okay, I am fully conscious of what is happening to me. You might think that is a good thing, but that is a different kind of battle altogether to watch myself deteriorate to a lump of flesh and bones, where I lose control of all my faculties.

You wouldn't believe what a personal culture shock this is for me. I have always been so self-sufficient and now I am dependent for all my personal care and needs on Zuzanna and Ksenija, who are doing all they can to make me comfortable.

It is so hard to face these physical realities. Sometimes I feel like Job in the Bible, but I know I have much more comforts and moral support than he had. Job even lost his children and I can say that my children are doing what they can to be here for me. I would like to believe in a double restoration like Job had, but sometimes I feel my faith is so weak.

I am so thankful for the friends that come by to see me. I know many are praying for me and I can feel it. I do know this. I have had a blessed life and I thank God for the friends and family I have learned so much from.

· · · · · ·

EPILOGUE

Jerry Low finished his race and met Jesus face to face on November 15, 2021.